I0815402

The PRESERVER'S GARDEN

Quarto.com

First Published in 2026 by Cool Springs Press, an imprint of The Quarto Group,
100 Cummings Center, Suite 265-D, Beverly, MA 01915, USA.
T (978) 282-9590 F (978) 283-2742

EEA Representation, WTS Tax d.o.o.,
Žanova ulica 3, 4000 Kranj, Slovenia.
www.wts-tax.si

Cool Springs Press titles are also available at discount for retail, wholesale, promotional, and bulk purchase. For details, contact the Special Sales Manager by email at specialsales@quarto.com or by mail at The Quarto Group, Attn: Special Sales Manager, 100 Cummings Center, Suite 265-D, Beverly, MA 01915, USA.

30 29 28 27 26 1 2 3 4 5

ISBN: 978-0-7603-9614-8

Digital edition published in 2026
eISBN: 978-0-7603-9615-5

Library of Congress Cataloging-in-Publication Data

Hill, Staci author | Hill, Jeremy (Farmer) author
The preserver's garden : how to grow a garden for fermenting, canning, pickling, dehydrating, freeze drying, and more / Staci & Jeremy Hill.
Beverly, MA : Cool Springs Press, 2026. | Includes bibliographical references and index.
LCCN 2025022209 (print) | LCCN 2025022210 (ebook) | ISBN 9780760396148 hardcover | ISBN 9780760396155 ebook
1. Canning and preserving--Handbooks, manuals, etc. 2. Plants, Edible--Preservation--Handbooks, manuals, etc. 3. Vegetable gardening--Handbooks, manuals, etc. 4. Food security
LCC TX601 .H65 2026 (print) | LCC TX601 (ebook) | DDC 641.4/2--dc23/eng/20250618

Design: Laura Shaw Design
Cover Image: Staci and Jeremy Hill
Page Layout: Marissa Mikolaities
Photography: Staci and Jeremy Hill, except page 202 by Brandon Martinez
Illustration: Jenna Lechner

Printed in Guangdong, China TT072025

Disclaimer

Home food preservation and canning must be performed according to the most up-to-date safety standards. The reader is encouraged to rely on two primary sources for this information: 1) The latest published and online notices from national, regional, and local departments of food and agriculture, and extension services; and 2) The most-recent safety guidelines provided by the manufacturers of the *specific* canning and preserving supplies that each reader is using. The recipes and other instructions in this book have been safely tested by the authors in their home kitchen, using their own equipment and supplies, in the course of writing this book, but they are not a replacement for the guidance given by the two sources named above. The authors and publisher disclaim any liability incurred as a consequence of the use and application of any of the contents of this book.

The PRESERVER'S GARDEN

HOW TO GROW A GARDEN FOR FERMENTING, CANNING, PICKLING, DEHYDRATING, FREEZE DRYING & MORE

Staci & Jeremy Hill

PLANNING YOUR PRESERVATION GARDEN

When you grow a garden with the intention of preserving food to eat year-round, you need to think beyond your immediate needs and beyond the convenience of going to the store to pick up what you need on a daily or weekly basis. There's a lot that goes into this part of the planning process. The first step is to figure out how much you already know.

If you're a meal planner, or you already have a working pantry, you've already done a good portion of this work. If you're the type who figures out what to make for dinner as you're starting to cook, or if you buy what looks good at the grocery store and figure out what to do with it later, then you may have more work ahead of you. Many of us start out somewhere in between.

Emergency Food versus a Working Pantry—What's the Difference?

A working pantry contains foods that you eat daily throughout the year. There are some food preservation methods, like freeze-drying or using Mylar bags and oxygen absorbers, that are great for creating long-term emergency food storage. Products created by canning and dehydrating have a more limited shelf life—it's best to eat through those items in one or two years and replace them when they're in season again. While this book will focus on foods you can grow and preserve yourself, it's important to remember that you can also fill gaps in your pantry with food purchased from the store, local farms, and farmers' markets.

What Are Your Goals?

To determine your goals for your food preservation pantry, you first need to think about what your family likes to eat. You may need to consider changing some of your habits as well. We eat things from our garden that we've never

WORKING PANTRY

A working pantry contains basic supplies and ingredients—it's like having your own mini-grocery store in your house. With a working pantry, your shopping and preserving lists will be based not on what you need to eat that week, but on what you need to have on hand to make diverse meals at any time.

A working pantry contains basic supplies and ingredients—it's like having your own mini-grocery store in your house. With a working pantry, your shopping and preserving lists will be based not on what you need to eat that week, but on what you need to have on hand to make diverse meals at any time.

← Tomatoes ripening on the counter in the pantry

purchased from a store, so if something sounds interesting, is easy to grow, or fills a gap, work it into your food preservation plan. Start by making a list of what you eat in a week. If you make grocery lists and meal plans, this may be easy. Include meals out at restaurants and determine whether you'd still need to eat out if you had preserved food on hand that was easy to prepare and eat.

QUESTIONS TO ASK WHEN DETERMINING HOW MUCH TO GROW TO MEET YOUR PRESERVATION GOALS

How Many Meals Do You Want to Cook Per Week?

In our go-go-go world, it's not uncommon for families to eat at restaurants or to eat takeout several times a week. Before we lived on our farm, we probably ate close to half of our meals out. At the time, it was just normal; now, looking back, it seems crazy. While these days we almost never eat food we don't prepare (maybe a handful of times per year), we didn't go from A to Z quickly. It was a gradual progression as we got better at growing, preserving, and preparing our own meals.

What Ingredients Can You Grow or Preserve for These Meals?

Think about all the ingredients for the meals your family enjoys and which ones are possible for you to grow in your climate. You may want to look at the produce profiles section on page 86 in this book to learn more about what you could grow yourself. If you're unsure, take a trip to your local farmers' market or community garden to see what other farmers and gardeners in your area are growing. Don't be afraid to ask questions! Most producers at local markets are happy to share their experiences and practices.

Do You Want to Increase the Variety of Vegetables and Fruits Your Family is Eating?

I'm guessing your answer is "yes!" because you've picked up a book that's connected to growing your own food and seasonal eating.

Do You Want to Preserve More Herbs or Seasonings?

A common complaint I hear from people who have dabbled in preserving their own food is that the food is bland. Part of this is because we're conditioned to eat over-salted foods that are mass-produced or prepared in restaurants. Another reason is that foods are often preserved without herbs or spices that can add flavor.

Would you Eat More Jam on Toast or PB&J If You Preserved the Jam or Jelly Yourself?

In our experience, you and your family are more likely to eat what you have on hand if you've grown and preserved it yourself. You know how much work went into growing and making that jam or jelly, so the rewards taste sweeter and you're less likely to waste what you have.

Once you've answered some of these questions, you can start to plan your preserver's garden.

MAKING THE CALCULATIONS

Let's say, for example, that your family loves pasta with tomato sauce and you want to eat it once a week. If you usually buy tomato sauce from the store, look at the ingredients and see what flavors you like. Most store-bought sauce has tomatoes, salt, and herbs or seasonings. Some of these sauces have added sugar, but consider a recipe without added sugar, as homegrown tomatoes or tomatoes purchased in season from a local farm tend to be naturally sweet. In fact, many people who can tomato sauce for the first time are turned off by it because they think it tastes too sweet: that's because they're adding unnecessary sugar to their already sweet tomatoes.

In this example you need to grow enough tomatoes for one jar of sauce per week for fifty weeks (consider that for some time in the summer you'll both be preserving and you'll have fresh sauce). You also need to grow enough basil to season the sauce. You can dry the basil separately or preserve it by adding it directly to the sauce with the tomatoes.

Our favorite recipe for tomato sauce with basil, shown in the sidebar on page 16, uses 20 pounds (9 kg) of tomatoes and results in 4 quarts (3.8 L) of sauce, which will be enough to feed your family with one month of pasta with tomato sauce meals. To reach your goal of one meal for fifty weeks of the year, you'll need approximately 230 pounds (104 kg) of tomatoes per year.

See the tomato plant profile on page 87 for more on how many tomato plants and what varieties you can grow to give your family a harvest they can use to preserve this much sauce per year.

A tray of tomatoes, ready to be planted

GROWING GOALS

FOOD	WEIGHT PER QUART	QUARTS PER WEEK	GOAL TO GROW
Tomatoes	3–5 pounds (1.4–2.3 kg)	1 quart (946 ml)	120–200 pounds (54–91 kg)
Green beans	2 pounds (907 g)	2 quarts (1.9 L)	160 pounds (73 kg)
Cucumbers	1–2 pounds (454–907 g)	½ quart (470 ml)	20–40 pounds (9.1–18 kg)

Storage Varieties, Preservation Varieties, and Multipurpose Varieties

Some varieties of vegetables are best for storage and others are best for preservation. There are also multipurpose varieties that fit both categories.

STORAGE VARIETIES

For many fruits and vegetables, you can reduce the amount needed to preserve by growing varieties bred for storage. Storage can be both long-term—longer than a growing season—and short-term—storing food until you can eat it or until the next season comes around and you can grow it again.

OUR FAVORITE TOMATO SAUCE

Tomato sauce in our pantry

Yield: 4 quarts or 8 pints (3.8 L)

INGREDIENTS

Approximately 20 pounds (9 kg) tomatoes
¼ cup (10 g) chopped fresh basil
1 cup (160 g) finely diced onion, optional
Chopped garlic, up to 8 cloves, optional
Salt to taste

INSTRUCTIONS

FOR SMOOTH SAUCE, place whole, stemless tomatoes (remove the cores if you prefer) in a high-powered blender. Blend until smooth. Add to a stock pot and cook down to desired consistency on a simmer (you'll end up with 30 to 50 percent of the original volume depending on the initial moisture in the tomato and your preferences), add basil and salt.

IF YOU PREFER A CHUNKY SAUCE, blanch, peel, and roughly chop the tomatoes instead of blending them. Add to a stock pot and cook to desired consistency on a simmer, add basil and salt.

Add the onions and garlic and cook. You can sauté the onions first or dice and add them to the sauce. Blend the garlic and onions with the tomatoes if a completely smooth sauce is desired, or leave chunky per your tastes and preferences.

This recipe is very flexible; however, for canning safety, **do** *measure your ingredients* if you're including onions and garlic. Garlic and onions are low acid and, therefore, adding too much (more than mentioned in the recipe) can lower the acidity of your sauce, making it unsafe for water-bath canning. Sauce can also be frozen in jars, vacuum bags, or other freezer-safe containers. If freezing, you can season the sauce to taste, as you do not need to worry about acidity and canning safety.

For water-bath canning, add 2 tablespoons (30 ml) lemon juice or ½ teaspoon citric acid per quart (946 ml); half of that if you are making pints. Process pint jars (473 ml) for 35 minutes and quart jars (946 ml) for 40 minutes (see page 68 for water-bath canning instructions).

Long-Term Storage

When we talk about long-term storage, sometimes that means keeping the whole fruit or vegetable in its natural form for a long time by choosing the right variety and providing a stable storage environment (think cured winter squash and onions). Other times, it means using preservation methods that alter the vegetable in order to make it suitable for long-term storage (think freeze-drying).

Storing vegetables in a natural state requires the right storage conditions. Winter squash, onions, and potatoes are some of the best foods you can grow for natural storage. With foods like these, your space, when combined with planting storage varieties of these foods, can help extend shelf life so that you don't need to "preserve" them—at least not right away. These foods don't require a root cellar (see page 67) if kept in a cool, dark space and, when properly cured, they can last months.

Here are some insights on specific vegetables good for natural-state storage.

- **MATURE WINTER SQUASH,** such as butternut, tromboncino squash/zucchino rampicante, 'Seminole' pumpkin, and 'Long Island Cheese' pumpkin will last between nine months to a year at room temperature. The key is combining the variety with allowing the squash to cure and fully mature on the vine. We typically do a fingernail test to tell if our winter squash is ready to harvest. If the skin on the winter squash is hard enough that you can't easily pierce it with your fingernail at the top near the stem, it's ready for harvest and storage. Some of these winter squash will still last four to six months even if they're harvested a little early, not quite cured or ripe.

How your food storage area looks will change throughout the year as you add, use, and replenish stock.

- **POTATOES,** such as the waxy 'Yukon Gold' or 'Kennebec' varieties, will have the longest storage life when kept in a cool, dry place. Starchier varieties such as russets have a shorter shelf life, so plan to eat those soon after harvest. Plant enough potatoes and you can harvest new potatoes one or two months before harvesting the mature crop; the mature crop will keep for around four months once dry and cured.

- **ONIONS** have a similar storage life. Their longevity really hinges on storage conditions. Keep them out of light and in cool temperatures or they'll think it's spring and grow new sprouts. Even if you don't grow storage varieties, curing the bulbs can extend their shelf life. We cure our onions by hanging or laying them on our covered porch until the leaves are completely dry. This usually takes a few weeks, then we move them to crates and store them indoors for four to six months. With a dark space, we could store our onions even longer, but four months is still one third of the year, which reduces the amount of onions we need to preserve. Also consider planting enough onions in March for you to have a good crop by May, when you can harvest small onions that are still large enough for cooking. Planting enough onions means harvesting green onions in April to June, small fresh onions in May to June, and harvesting and curing our mature onions in late June. So from April to October we don't need to use preserved onions from our food storage. When you calculate how many onions you need to store for the year, you only need to preserve enough for six months.

TOMATO CONSIDERATIONS

There are true old Italian varieties of tomatoes that can hang out in your pantry for months at room temperature—and then there are modern varieties bred for shipping and long shelf life. In the case of modern varieties bred for shipping and shelf life, the tomatoes tend to have a thicker skin and usually lack the depth of flavor found in many heirloom tomato varieties.

Roma types and San Marzano sauce tomatoes offer a happy medium: they keep longer than meaty heirloom slicers, giving you more time to preserve them and allow more to ripen. If you're growing tomatoes in your own backyard garden, you don't need them to store and ship.

AN ALL-IN STRATEGY

While the focus of this book is garden produce preservation, which is a great place to start, an all-in food preservation strategy should eventually include most foods your family consumes regularly. For us, this includes beans, grains, and meats. The preservation methods for these items can be as varied as garden produce and would require another book to go into the necessary detail for each.

We include them here at a high level to put them in the back of your mind as you start thinking about food preservation.

If you have access to a root cellar, you can expand your long-term storage for natural-state vegetables even further. First, determine what type of cellar you have and what type of storage various foods need; some need dry storage and some need 80 to 90 percent humidity. Vegetables like onions, garlic, shallots, winter squash, and sweet potatoes do better in cool, dark, dry conditions at 50 to 70 percent humidity, while potatoes, carrots, radishes, beets, and turnips require cool, damp storage. We don't have a root cellar or damp storage space, so our food storage is all kept at room temperature in normal household humidity (higher in the summer, lower in the winter).

Other than a couple of spells of extreme cold in the winter, we have an enclosed porch that, with a bit of insulation (blankets on the windows), we can keep at around 40°F (4.4°C). This gives us a dry walk-in storage area that extends the shelf life of our winter squash, potatoes, onions, and apples. Get creative with your spaces! Sometimes you can close off a back bedroom to create a space that's cooler for storing produce through the winter months. If that isn't possible, potatoes and apples can be kept in a refrigerator, if the humidity is adjusted accordingly (which can be tricky).

These foods with a natural shelf-life of over one season are the exception rather than the rule, so through the rest of this book we'll look at foods that require more extraordinary measures to ensure multiseason use.

Even with a root cellar or an enclosed porch, you may need to further extend the storage life of your vegetables. That's when you can start pressure canning, freezing, dehydrating, or freeze-drying them.

For a more shelf-stable approach, and for things that don't otherwise store well in a natural state—tomatoes, peppers, berries, and fruits—canning, dehydrating, and freezing are great options. When you're really bringing in large harvests, freezing and then later canning or dehydrating is

VERY LONG-TERM STORAGE FOR SEASON REPLACEMENT AND EMERGENCIES

Having food security, regardless of outside events, provides a sense of security and well-being.

Generally, people engage in very long-term storage for one or both of the following reasons.

SEASON REPLACEMENT

We use season replacement preservation for our tomatoes. In general, we plan on our harvest either failing or doing poorly at least once every five years or so. To ensure food security (in this case, a ready supply of tomato sauce), we try to have what we plan to use over the course of two years on the pantry shelves at any time, so we can absorb a bad year in the garden without changing the way we eat. Generally, this will mean finding a food preservation method that lasts two to three years. This can be translated for nearly every type of food you grow.

EMERGENCIES

Supply chain disruptions, social unrest, natural or manmade catastrophes, and war are some of the reasons people want to have food that can last for years available on their shelves. There are methods of preservation that can keep your food in stasis for twenty-five or more years, but you really need a plan in place to consume the food on a rotating basis (eating the oldest food as you add new). These strategies can be expanded from the garden to the grocery store, by vacuum-sealing, freeze-drying, and oxygen-starving many foods you typically buy at the store to further increase their shelf life.

a great way to keep up. For example, if you plant regular heirloom slicing tomatoes that don't stay fresh for more than a few days and you can only preserve your tomatoes on the weekends, be sure to leave some room in your freezer. You'll need to freeze your fresh-picked tomatoes until you have time to can them. With ample freezer space, you'll be able to "freeze time" when it comes to your tomato harvest.

Short-Term Storage

Short-term food storage means storing food until you can eat it or until the next season when you can grow it again. Essentially, it's storage for one season or less. Short-term storage can take the form of canning, freezing, dehydrating, or simply curing foods. Later sections of this book will focus on these and a handful of other food preservation methods, including the necessary equipment and potential pros and cons.

All the considerations we've discussed in this chapter will play a role in planning your food preservation garden and scheduling the time it will take to put up the harvest. While some preservation methods are versatile, your lifestyle, preferences, and storage space will have an impact on your preservation goals.

← Dual-purpose spaces can be your friend. In summer, we ripen tomatoes on shelves in the pantry.

→ Keep in mind your storage space when deciding on short- and long-term plans.

URBAN GARDENING VERSUS HOMESTEAD GARDENING

If you've picked up this book, chances are good you're interested in gardening and growing your own food, and you likely already have a garden. You're probably wondering if you have enough space to grow food to preserve. The answer is, any size garden can become a food preservation garden.

Whether you're gardening on a balcony, in a suburban yard, in a community garden, or have acres of space, you can do it! Gardening for food preservation has more to do with your goals for the garden than with the amount of space you have available.

If you're gardening indoors, on a balcony, or in a very small space, we recommend looking into community gardens in your area. Many neighborhoods and cities have community garden plots you can rent (sometimes at no cost) to grow food. If there isn't a community garden in your area, consider working with a local business, place of worship, or your city parks to develop a new community garden program.

The size of your garden should represent a blend of your short- and long-term food storage goals.

Advice for Both Large- and Small-Space Gardeners

Here are some considerations and planning techniques to keep in mind as you develop your preservation garden, whatever its size.

BE SELECTIVE

When growing food for preservation, especially in a small space, there are often plants that make sense to grow and others that don't. There may be vegetables or fruits you really enjoy eating, but perhaps they would be more practical to source from a local farmer or farmers' market.

For us, green beans always make sense to grow. In our area they're priced higher at local markets and even auctions, likely because they take time to harvest. We don't have a lot of pests that harm green beans, making it an easy decision to grow them (we'll talk more about green bean considerations and how to fit them into your garden in our produce profiles section).

↖ Small raised beds can produce more food than most people think.

↑ A larger garden requires more people power and can be a great way to involve the whole family.

← When growing your own food, plan for bringing in smaller amounts of food at a time.

Tomatoes are also a good choice to grow because the tomatoes sold at markets aren't usually the varieties with the best flavor, and they're priced higher. If you need a lot of tomatoes for sauce, it may be a better choice to buy a bulk box of canning tomatoes from your local market and then make diced or stewed tomatoes from what you grow. Tomatoes sold at markets as canners are usually tomatoes with imperfections that either don't matter at all or can be cut off when making sauce. They often need to be processed quickly before they degrade further, so keep this in mind if you purchase them.

Getting a workable amount of tomato sauce takes a lot of tomatoes. In fact, we've been told not to make our own tomato sauce because it's easier to buy premade at the store—as you may have guessed, though, we strongly disagree with this position! We focus on growing all our own tomatoes because it's something we've worked up to over the years. Tomatoes are the one produce we can grow—in all its forms—for the entire year. We doubled the number of tomato plants we grew in 2024 in an effort to put in less work for more tomatoes. It worked. You can fit a *lot* of tomato plants in a relatively small space compared to things like winter squash.

Speaking of squash, we try to grow winter squash every year because we know it will keep without processing or preserving. Bear in mind that one winter squash plant grown on a trellis takes up the same amount of space as two tomato plants and only produces around two winter squash (one exception to this is butternut squash which may produce four to six squash per plant). We'll talk about using trellises as a space-saving technique for growing in chapter 5.

Produce like summer squash, potatoes, and onions tend to be more affordable at farmers' markets, making it reasonable to save precious garden space and purchase those items instead of growing them. Summer squash pests can be intense and highly destructive in a small garden, while larger producers tend to have less pest pressure. Purchasing pickling cucumbers for pickles or relish may also make more sense than growing them in a small garden. The best pickles are made from cucumbers processed the day they are picked: purchasing a bulk bag or box of pickling cucumbers from a local farmer will give you more cucumbers, which will be ready at the same time, than if you grew your own in a small space. Later in this chapter, we'll offer additional advice on outsourcing produce for preservation.

This all translates to being mindful about how you use your space, particularly if that space is limited.

ROTATE YEAR BY YEAR

Another way to maximize your garden is to rotate what you grow and use more long-term storage methods to build up your food storage, such as freeze-drying; this is especially true if you grow in a small space. Though this may not be the most balanced approach, it can be effective if you're growing produce that you'll always want on hand.

Here's an example of how this could work.

If you dedicate your garden to growing tomatoes in year one and then grow three (or more) years' worth of tomatoes, then do the same thing in year two with peppers, in years three and after you'll have plenty of both tomatoes and peppers in storage—but you might have trouble making them into salsa. A more well-rounded approach would be to focus on growing extras of one crop each year, then rotate to a new crop each season. You'll still be growing smaller amounts of everything you'd like to eat and preserve, with the addition of one extra crop each year. If you're using a freeze-dryer, this approach makes even more sense because what you freeze-dry can be shelf stable for twenty or more years. Also, freeze-dried tomatoes and peppers are great for salsa, and you can even can it later if you want. The only limits are your imagination and your plans when it comes to this type of strategy. Using this rotation method in conjunction with supplementing from other growers, you can meet your goals much faster than with traditional gardening practices. This is also an effective strategy for building a stock of long-term emergency food over time while still growing for daily use.

USE THE PROPER SPACING

It may be tempting to plant extra plants, especially if your garden is a small space. While plant-spacing advice listed on seed packets is just a guideline, extreme overplanting will reduce yields and increase the chance of disease.

Rather than overcrowding and overplanting, practices such as companion planting, interplanting, planting high-yield varieties, succession planting, and even pruning and vertical growing can help you make the most of your space.

COMPANION PLANTING AND INTERPLANTING

Companion planting focuses on leveraging the strengths and weaknesses of certain plants to create synergy and offer mutual benefits for whatever plants you're partnering together. This is a space saver with added benefits, from providing shade or extending the harvest to preventing disease or repelling pests.

Interplanting and companion planting overlap quite a bit. Interplanting is a simple way to squeeze more plants into your available space. Interplanting sometimes involves companion planting principles, but it also partners plants based on factors like growth habits and root depth to maximize your use of space.

An example of interplanting and companion planting is placing basil and peppers together because they have similar needs and growth habits—practically speaking, basil plants can help hold up the mature pepper plants once they become heavy with fruit—and these two plants can often be harvested at the same time. Both have a reputation for loving heat, but neither likes the full sun when it's over 85°F (29°C). They prefer a bit of late-day shade, so you can put them both in the same conditions. If you don't have a late-day shade spot for your peppers, consider planting them with eggplant, which can help shade its neighbors with its bigger leaves, sheltering and cooling them.

Consider root growth and water needs as well. For example, don't plant rosemary, which prefers to be dry, with something like squash, which needs daily water.

Another thing to consider with companion planting: the life stages of various plants and using their differences to your advantage. On our farm, we don't typically plant our tomato starts (a.k.a., transplants) in the ground until the first part of May. By square footage, a large percentage

← Onions and tomatoes partner well when planted in the same space.

of our garden space is taken up by tomatoes, so we plant other crops in that same space before the tomatoes need it, even if there is some overlap.

Our favorite items to plant with tomatoes are onions and sugar snap peas. Both are planted earlier in the spring (or late winter). The peas are nearing the end of their productive life by the time the tomato starts are ready to go into the ground. If you grow dwarf pea varieties, the tomatoes will quickly outgrow them and even shade the peas, prolonging their production. If you grow taller pea varieties, you may need to remove the vines before they've finished producing to avoid shading the tomatoes early in their growth. The onions protect the tiny tomato plants when they're first planted, and they help shield the tomatoes from spring storms while they become established. The onions also repel many of the bugs that like to feed on baby tomatoes.

PLANTING HIGH-YIELDING VARIETIES

Another space-saving technique is planting high-yield varieties. While they can be beautiful and pack a lot of flavor, some varieties just aren't heavy producers. When you can grow one hundred plants this isn't a problem, but if you're limited in space and can only grow five plants, you want to make the most of that space by choosing varieties that produce more yields.

Planting a high-yield variety of bush beans, for example, can be much more effective than planting a pretty heirloom variety. We love heirloom 'Dragon's Tongue' beans, but these plants aren't high producers when compared with something like yellow wax beans or 'Blue Lake' bush beans. Some bush beans are more heat tolerant as well (and 'Dragon's Tongue' beans aren't one of them). Heat-tolerant beans will keep producing in the summer, whereas other varieties don't do well with temperatures over 85°F (29°C). Beans are self-pollinating and, when temperatures get too high, some varieties won't produce as many pods and may even produce abnormally shaped beans. Because of this, we plant a few different bean varieties every year to hedge our bets. We love to eat the 'Dragon's Tongue' beans, but we don't rely on them to meet our preservation goals.

Green beans are a plant that, depending on your climate, can be planted multiple times throughout the growing season.

SUCCESSION PLANT TO MAXIMIZE SPACE AND PRODUCTION

Succession planting means planting multiple rounds of the same or a similar crop to take advantage of a plant's limited harvest period, and to repeat the growing process multiple times throughout a single growing season. It's a valuable practice that can maximize your harvest and take advantage of planting in the same ground multiple times.

Succession planting can be done in two different ways.

- Plant a new planting of the same crop over and over.
- Replace a spring crop with a summer crop, or a summer crop with a fall crop.

Most good candidates for succession planting have a shorter life cycle and faster maturation rate. On the next page are some crops to consider for succession planting, based on their preferred season of growth.

If you don't like radishes, it might be because you've never had them fresh from the garden.

Cool Season Succession Crops

RADISHES. Plant more seeds once a week throughout the spring, starting very early. Once temperatures are over 85°F (29°C), the plants will start to bolt (go to flower) and won't make big radishes. With proper succession planting, though, you can get a lot of radishes in a limited amount of space during the cooler spring months.

LETTUCE. Consider a weekly succession planting throughout the spring. You can also companion plant by planting lettuce near taller crops (like tomatoes) to provide shade as the weather warms. Replant again in the fall.

SPINACH, KALE, SWISS CHARD, BOK CHOY. All of these cool season lovers can be planted like lettuce. We direct sow their seeds, but be aware that each of these crops has a different space requirement. For example, spinach can be sown thickly, with the seeds almost touching each other, but bok choy and Swiss chard need more room to grow—several inches, in the case of bok choy—and this is also the case with some varieties of kale.

BEETS. Beets like cool to moderate temperatures but don't thrive in temperatures above 80°F (27°C). Make sure to leave several inches between seeds to allow plenty of room for the roots to grow.

CARROTS. Plant weekly, much like radishes, through spring, summer, and fall. Carrots are unique in that their roots will continue growing if the conditions are to their liking. We've forgotten to harvest spring carrots some years, which resulted in a monster-sized harvest in the fall!

PEAS. We love snap peas, and plant them as a predecessor to our tomatoes to take advantage of the trellises that aren't being used by the tomatoes in the spring (more on this strategy on page 30). We then plant snap peas again in the fall somewhere else in the garden, after the cucumbers and pole beans are done. They can be prolific as long as the temperatures aren't too high.

TURNIPS. Direct sow in the spring and fall, much like beets.

Warm Season Succession Crops

GREEN BEANS. Plant bean seeds on your last frost date in the spring and again eight weeks before your first frost date of the fall. If you live somewhere with cooler summers but still have a long enough growing season, you can plant a midsummer succession crop as well. Most bush varieties of green beans do not develop beans when the temperatures get above about 85°F (29°C)—they really like weather around 75°F (24°C).

CUCUMBERS. We plant monthly successions in May, June, and July. Plant your last succession two-and-a-half to three months before your first frost date.

ZUCCHINI. Treat zucchini like cucumbers. If pest pressure gets too high, it may be best to skip a succession and take a month off to let the pests leave or die before starting a new crop. Many gardeners plant zucchini in the spring and again in the summer. If you can keep *all* members of the Cucurbit family out of your garden in the spring (including pumpkins, cucumbers, winter squash, etc.), you can then plant them later in the summer, around the first of July for us, and avoid pests that way. The theory is that any overwintered squash bugs and squash vine borers will have moved on by then. Personally, we like to start zucchini seeds in the greenhouse two to four weeks early and get ahead of the pests by having more mature plants go out into the garden in the spring. Then we pull those plants out when they die in late July or early August and wait a few weeks before planting new summer squash plants in a different area of the garden. Squash bugs are sneaky!

TOMATOES. You can succession plant tomatoes in some areas. For us, in southern Missouri, we can plant tomato starts from early May all the way through July 1 and get a plentiful harvest before frost. An early July planting of a 6-inch (15 cm) tall tomato start gives us three-and-a-half months until the arrival of our average first frost. In the years we've done this, the tomato harvest was in late August to September, with a lot of green tomatoes ready for storage when the first frost hit (for us, the average first frost is in early October). Our May-planted tomatoes are usually done by mid-August or early September from the excessive heat and disease that's typical of our humid climate.

Growing green beans can be feast or famine.

SPEAKING OF GREEN TOMATOES

You can intentionally harvest green tomatoes—or just harvest everything on the vine—before the first frost.

We usually plan for green tomatoes at the end of the season. While most people know about fried green tomatoes, green tomatoes in general are a great ingredient in baked goods, such as green tomato spice cake, green tomato muffins, and green tomato false apple cobbler or pie. We also like to make green tomato jam and pickled green tomatoes. You'll find more on this in chapter 5.

More Succession Planting Tips

Here are some of our favorite strategies for effective succession planting. They're equally as useful in small spaces as they are in our large garden.

SUCCESSION TIP 1. With summer squash, green beans, and cucumbers, we like to plant quick-maturing varieties with some varieties maturing in just forty-five to fifty days, meaning you can be harvesting in less than two months! If your growing season goes from May to October like ours, that is a six-month-long growing season. Using fast-maturing varieties, we can plant three successions of summer squash and cucumbers. Bush green beans don't pollinate well in the heat, so they often don't produce at the peak of summer temperatures. We plant fast-maturing bush bean varieties in the spring and again in the fall. We direct sow our green bean seeds the first week of May for harvesting in late June and early July, and then we sow more in early to mid-August for a mid-September to mid-October harvest (before frost strikes!).

Planting seed potatoes can be fun, allowing you to plant many varieties side by side.

SUCCESSION TIP 2. We plant seed potatoes in our potato bed in March and harvest them in July, leaving the space empty for over half of the growing season. We typically rake and mulch the area to prep it for a fall bean succession planting. We've found that the beans really like following the potatoes, because the ground is loose and easy for the baby bean plants to take root. The beans, in turn, leave a high amount of nitrogen in the soil, which next year's potatoes thrive on.

SUCCESSION TIP 3. We plant pole beans in May at the same time as bush beans. They mature later, giving us more beans to harvest in July and August when the bush beans are between successions.

SUCCESSION TIP 4. Partner tomatoes with peas (shelling, snow, or sugar snap) when you succession plant. We've already mentioned employing this strategy on our tomato trellises, but here's how you do it.

- Peas are a crop you can grow in the spring on a trellis; they decline in the heat and, depending on when that happens, they can produce into July or be completely done and dying by early June. Either way, start when the pea plants are ready to be removed.
- Don't pull the pea plants out, just cut them off at the base, leaving the roots to decompose and feed the soil. We feed the plants to our animals—chickens, pigs, and goats all love them—which gives us the incentive to take them out of the garden before they're completely dead and toasted.
- Then plant your late-season tomatoes along the same trellis and off you go!

Depending on the sunlight situation in your garden, you can even interplant tomatoes with mature pea plants. We tried to do that with an early May planting of tomatoes and it didn't work out so well because the peas created too much shade for the tomato plants to thrive. However, if it had been a month or two later, the same tomato plants might have appreciated the shade and protection.

It can take some time to figure out how to use your space and what works for your garden.

PLAN AHEAD

There are many things to consider when using these strategies in your garden. Plan ahead according to what you want to grow, but be prepared to adjust your plan based on what's happening. If you plan to put out a second succession of tomatoes in early June but your peas are having a great year, be prepared to pot up those tomato starts and wait a bit to put them out in the garden, *or* find a new spot for them (or maybe combine the two by potting up half and planting the other half in a new space).

There are always other options—think of your garden like a puzzle or a game of Tetris. Try your best to predict the new spaces that will open up and have a plan for the next thing you'll plant there.

The "Space-Is-Not-an-Issue" Garden: Considerations for Large Gardens

Even if you aren't constrained by space, pay attention to the time and potential money it takes to plant, maintain, and harvest a large garden. Sometimes it makes more sense to stay small to keep things manageable. On our farm, we have all the space available we could ever want for gardening, but anything over the approximately half-acre we currently use would provide diminishing returns. The general maintenance of more space would be less efficient for us. Naturally, everyone's needs, tolerance, labor availability, and budget are different.

When determining how big a space you're going to garden, consider the following.

Labor

How many people will be gardening the area and how much time can each person dedicate over the season? In reality, the maintenance of a one-acre mixed vegetable garden would be considered a full-time job for just one person. And that just means weeding, planting, and harvesting—not preserving what you produce. Without plans for operating a market garden, most people very likely do not need to grow on more than one acre.

Budget

Your garden budget should include soil amendments, compost, mulch, tools, weed fabric, tarps, trellis-building materials, fencing, and anything else you might need to purchase. Add in whatever tools you may need (see below). That's not including your time. In some areas, water cost may also be a factor. If you're working with a large space, you'll need to budget for cover crops to feed and cover the soil when it's not in production.

Tools

Do you have a tractor or a tiller? Or do you have hand tools like a hoe, shovel, and a rake?

Fencing

How will you keep pests like deer, squirrels, racoons—or even human neighbors—from invading or destroying your garden? The answers will be specific to your area, but whatever your needs you should think carefully about this, as fencing can be very expensive. In our area, we need to keep out small animals like rabbits, as well as deer and other large animals. We place an eight-foot (2.4 m) tall fence that can keep the deer out and add two feet (61 cm) of chicken wire at the bottom to repel rabbits and other small critters. Accounting for posts, the cost of fencing our garden is over $3 USD per linear foot (0.3 m).

DON'T FORGET TO FEED YOUR SOIL

When you're intensively planting by using succession planting and interplanting, especially in a small garden, you'll have more success if the garden is properly supported. While some companion and succession planting strategies can help you reach this goal (see the section on page 30 about potatoes and green beans), you'll probably need to amend the soil throughout the growing season. Remember that every fruit and vegetable that comes out of your garden requires fuel to grow, and that fuel comes in the form of sunlight, water, and soil nutrients. While you can't necessarily control the sunlight, you can keep your garden properly watered (we'll discuss this on page 40)—it's up to you to replenish depleted soil nutrients for the highest yields your garden can produce.

While you can add purchased amendments to your soil, be aware that bagged manure, bagged compost, and commercial fertilizers, and other amendments you can buy in a store can do more harm than good. Quality control is often lax with these products, and labeling requirements tend to be loosely regulated. These amendments can also be contaminated with herbicides, and bagged manure and compost are sometimes full of filler like wood chips and sand.

We've had the best luck using manure and compost that comes from our own farm, but we realize this may not be an option for most people. When possible, get your soil amendments from a local supplier and ask the person or company how it was made and what kinds of ingredients (including fertilizers or pesticides) have been used in its production.

If you have room for a compost pile, get one started right now. Compost is the best all-around soil amendment, and adding it to your garden between succession plantings and at the start of each new gardening season goes a long way toward depleting any nutrients lost during the prior growth cycle.

Our go-to fertilizer is rabbit manure: We keep rabbits just for this purpose. Their waste is a wonderful fertilizer, as it breaks down quickly and won't burn your plants if you lay it down fresh, instead of resting or composting it. It's still manure, though, for safety apply this manure at least 120 days before you plan on harvesting vegetables that make contact with the soil or could be splashed with the fertilizer. For vegetables (and fruits) that do not touch the soil, manure should be applied ninety days before harvest.

We typically top-dress our beds with manure in the fall or late winter. This complies with the National Organics Standards Board's rules for manure use, and if you follow this guide you won't have to track temperatures in the compost pile to make sure it gets hot enough. Rabbit manure will not harm your flowers or decorative plants. The rule of thumb is, if you're not eating it, you don't need to worry about pathogens.

Goat, sheep, and alpaca manure works the same way as rabbit droppings. Consider making friends with a local farmer and get your manure for free, or perhaps exchange it for a basket of your produce. Consider how you'll use it when you look for a source of manure.

Manure from cows, horses, and chickens is also widely available, but these will have to be composted or aged to avoid burning your plants. These manures also contain more nitrogen, which means that, even when applied in the fall and allowed to overwinter and age the appropriate amount of time, they'll support growing more leaves and fewer flowers. This is good for bushy greens, but for tomatoes and peppers you want more flowers. Another concern with high-nitrogen manure is that it can lead to aphid problems for your tomatoes and peppers. Manure from livestock can be great for your soil, but give it ample time to rest before they touch your plants, and a little goes a long way—avoid overdoing it.

Bunnies and goats are the unsung heroes of our farm. They're the only animals whose poop we look forward to!

If the manure has hay mixed in, be prepared for weeds. Composting at high temperatures can help eliminate viable weed seeds; we mulch with old hay and the weeds are manageable with weed fabric, so don't let this scare you! On our farm, we face the challenge of keeping up with turning compost and being unsure when it's ready. Counting back 90 or 120 days and letting the manure rest in place has been easier and works especially well with our no-till beds.

EXTENSION SERVICES

If you live in the United States, your local county agricultural extension office may offer free or low-cost soil testing resources. Follow their report's guidelines for what you need to added to your soil (or in some cases, what needs to be removed or reduced), but also bear in mind what you want to plant in the area that was tested. Soil test recommendations are often generalized to get the soil to a more neutral point in order to support the broadest number of vegetables; that means the tests don't necessarily offer specific recommendations for individual crops. You may, for example, want to add extra nitrogen to the area where your greens will be growing but not to the area where you have strawberries, which have lower nitrogen requirements. If you're just starting out, think of a soil report as your guide instead of rules you must follow as you plan your garden.

Cattle panels are a go-to in our garden. They can be put on posts for tomatoes or bent into arches for pumpkins and vining squash.

Trellising

Vegetable plants often require trellising. This includes tomatoes, vining beans, cucumbers, and many squash, among others. For example, when fruiting, a single indeterminate tomato plant with all its fruit can weigh as much a 50 pounds (23 kg). We plant four to six tomatoes (depending on the variety) on one 16-foot (4.9 m) long livestock panel held up by three 6-foot (1.8 m) tall T-posts. Each panel costs around $30 USD, and when you add $6 USD per post and the connecting hardware, our trellising system costs an average of almost $10 USD per tomato plant. This equipment can be used for several years, so it's a worthwhile investment, but the setup costs for fencing like this can be daunting. We've built up our infrastructure by investing in the equipment over several years.

What to Grow versus What to Buy

While it's easy to say, "I want to grow all of the food I consume," remember to set realistic goals and grow into them with time. Even on a show like *Little House on the Prairie*, the family still went to the general store to stock up on certain items. Gardening burnout from overcommitment is a common problem—especially for people just getting started.

We like to use a hybrid approach. We grow what makes sense and preserve it, but we also like to buy in bulk from places like Azure Standard and warehouse club stores, as well as from other local farms. We sometimes preserve these purchased items as well. We buy a lot of peaches and apples from local farmers and supplement our home-grown strawberries and pears to make our yearly stash of jams and jellies. We purchase grains in bulk and store them in vacuum-sealed bags until we're ready to mill them. And when organic rice goes on sale at our local warehouse club store, we stock up and store it in vacuum bags.

Some items are not worth trying to grow them yourself. Do you have space to grow your own grains and the equipment to process them? If you do, is it economical? Depending on your space and climate, it may make sense to buy produce like grains and corn from a supplier.

Canning and freeze-drying sweet corn is great, but we haven't had great luck growing it. There is a neighboring farm about 5 miles (8 km) from us where they grow the best tri-color sweet corn; we buy fifteen to twenty dozen ears a year from them and preserve it. This frees us up to grow what we know we can manage, while still keeping our pantry stocked.

Fruit and vegetables that don't grow well in your area, that you don't have space for, or that you haven't had time to establish may make sense to outsource. We like to purchase things grown as close to us as possible, since the further your fruits and vegetables have to travel to get to you, the more they will lose their nutrients. Preserving with produce grown in season by local farms helps with quality and nutrition. If you've ever eaten sweet corn the day it's picked, you know what we're talking about!

ORGANIC VERSUS CONVENTIONAL

If you opt to purchase a produce item instead of grow it yourself, there are many things to consider when choosing where you buy produce for preserving and stocking your pantry. We use all-organic methods in our garden, which is our preference, so when sourcing produce, we look to other organic growers and farmers first. We also like homemade, unprocessed ingredients instead of processed or mass-produced foods. We also value local produce that has traveled the least number of miles possible.

Apples are a good example. We can apple sauce, apple butter, apple jelly, and make our own apple cider vinegar each year, and we love freeze-dried and dehydrated apple slices as quick snacks. So do we grow our own apples? We planted an orchard eight years ago with five apple trees and, in theory, we should have had a couple hundred pounds of apples from our trees every year since the trees matured, for the past five years. This may have been possible in theory, and some areas might support a yield like that, but there are factors that make it difficult for us to grow our own apples.

Now, we have one remaining apple tree, and we've picked about ten apples from it in the eight years we've had it. The other trees could have lived, but we let our sheep graze in our orchard after six years of not getting any fruit. The sheep decided that apple bark was tasty, so they debarked and killed several of our apple trees. Apart from this damage, we live in a low-lying area, which allows cold air, especially in the spring and fall, to settle, bringing the temperature down as much as 15°F (–9°C). Other farmers and gardeners in our area can successfully grow certain fruits year after year, but that's not an option for us. Even neigh-

MICROCLIMATES

Do you live in a microclimate? The climate in these anomalous areas—sometimes measured in feet or hundreds of feet—can differ drastically from the land around it. This can be due to elevation, sunshine, wind patterns, or surrounding geography. We experience temperatures up to 15°F (–9°C) colder than properties even a mile away because of the topography of our land and the way the sun hits it when the trees don't have leaves. Consider possible microclimates in your planning.

Apples are hard to grow, so we augment them in our storage plans with bulk purchases.

bors a few hundred yards uphill have better luck with their fruit trees.

It's more practical for us to purchase apples, and when we do, we have a choice: local apples, semi-local apples, or organic apples from across the country? For day-to-day fresh eating, we buy organic apples available at the grocery store. For preservation, we try to purchase boxes of local or semi-local apples that are conventionally grown. We try to buy local organic apples when they're in stock.

This is just one of the factors that goes into every decision we make about the produce we buy for our food storage. The same type of decisions should go into purchasing any foods for preservation and storage.

PURCHASING PRODUCE IN BULK

Buying in bulk can be a great way to leapfrog progress toward your preservation goals. The hardest part about getting started with bulk-buying can be knowing where to find your produce. Here are some options, depending on your area.

Produce auctions are a great option to augment your food storage goals, depending on your area.

WAREHOUSE CLUBS. While pricing and availability may vary based on what is close to you, large warehouse clubs can be a great option for bulk purchasing. These are where many small restaurants get their produce, and the quality of product is usually top-notch.

GROCERY STORES. Consider developing a relationship with a local grocery store owner, manager, or produce manager. The produce departments of most grocery stores waste a huge amount because of spoilage, and often that produce gets thrown away or turned to compost. Talk to the store management and arrange to buy an extra case of something that won't sell; they can call you and sell it at a discount before the produce goes bad. This can be a win-win for everyone involved.

DISCOUNT STORES. In most areas, discount stores with grocery departments deal in expired or nearly expired grocery products. Several in our area bring in bulk shipments of seasonal fruits like apples, peaches, and strawberries. They sell the produce by the bushel at a fraction of grocery store prices. While produce like this is typically not organic, it's usually high quality and good for a mass canning session that can fill your pantry shelves.

RESTAURANT AND FOOD SERVICE SUPPLIERS. While these are typically wholesale-only operations, some have lax rules about selling to home canners. While you'll have to buy in bulk, this is a great option for high-quality, low-cost food. Consider developing a relationship with a local food service supplier and make it advantageous for them to sell to you, knowing that you'll be a small customer versus the larger operations that are their typical client.

PRODUCE AUCTIONS. One of our favorite ways to buy bulk produce is at local farm auctions. While the frequency of these auctions varies greatly by region, they're worth seeking out. Search online for county produce auctions in your area: auctions are more common than most people think. Ask at roadside produce stands or farmers' markets, and chances are good some of the vendors are reselling produce—or they know who does. At produce auctions you can often talk to the growers and find out about their growing practices. Generally, auctions require you to purchase in bulk (the results are different based on each seller); if you're purchasing for preservation, this can be the least expensive option for filling in gaps, and the produce usually comes straight off of the farm.

Develop Your Plan

With all these preservation garden planning thoughts in mind, develop a unique plan for your own space. Decide which crops and varieties to grow (and which to buy) and map out a planting plan that uses as many of the space- and yield-maximizing techniques outlined in this chapter as possible.

Next, let's explore the special considerations and methods needed to maintain your preservation garden to encourage healthy and productive plants.

MAINTAINING YOUR PRESERVATION GARDEN

Once you've decided what you're going to grow and preserve, it's time to set up and maintain your garden. Since the goal of a preservation garden is maximum production for preservation, rather than just harvesting a bit to have with dinner, this changes the maintenance strategy needed and separates it from the tending requirements of a small kitchen garden.

Care Tasks

As they get started, most gardeners struggle to keep up with garden care. Humans are routine-driven creatures: when something new is introduced that requires care and attention, it can be forgotten if it isn't carefully made part of our routine. Plants are passive, and they don't bug you for attention like a baby or a puppy. One sad lament I hear all too often is, "I forgot to check my plants for a few days, and when I did, they were all dead!"

In general, after your plants are in the ground, their care can be divided into easy-to-manage daily, weekly, and monthly maintenance tasks. We encourage you to ask these questions before you start: how do you organize your day? What methods can you include to help your garden remind you to complete the required tasks? Thankfully, we have smartphones that help us schedule reminders. If a physical note is more your style, you can pencil in garden care on your daily planner.

Guiding growing plants requires work, but when they thrive it's validation that your work is paying off.

DAILY TASKS

While you don't have to do everything every day, your garden is a collection of living things and, barring perfect conditions, it needs at least a little bit of attention every day. If you can't get to everything every day, don't let that keep you from working on your garden: going out to the garden daily for whatever amount of time you have makes a difference. You don't have to get it all done—set a timer, do what you can do, and leave the rest for tomorrow!

Daily Walk-Through

We make time for a daily walk-through in the morning and evening during gardening season. If your schedule allows, choose a cooler time of day when you may have a bit of shade to work in to accomplish tasks that may take a bit more time. For us, early mornings in the summer are great for this: the air is nice and cool, and there's nothing like the quiet tranquility of a morning garden stroll.

During a walk-through, spot-check for pest damage (holes, poop, wilted leaves), check the soil moisture (again, look for wilted leaves), tie up plants that need support, and direct vines back onto their trellises.

Harvesting

During peak growing season, harvesting is an important daily task. To get the most out of your garden, bring in produce every day, before the pests get it or it becomes too large. Tomatoes, beans, peas, cucumbers, and summer squash are examples of produce that needs to be harvested—or at least checked—daily.

Watering

With raised beds and container gardens, watering will be a daily task unless it rains consistently (see page 44 for more watering advice). Remember that raised beds will dry out more quickly than in-ground gardens. Setting up some kind of automated irrigation system can simplify your life when it comes to watering, especially if you're short on time.

↑ Harvesting doesn't always mean waiting until fruits and vegetables are ripe. Many varieties will continue to ripen once they blush (like these tomatoes).

→ Harvesting can also be done as a secondary task. If you see something that needs to be picked as you walk by, it's okay just to grab it.

A HELPFUL TIP

Find a gardening accountability buddy and share photos or texts about your garden during or after your daily walk-throughs. Remember that this relationship is symbiotic, and you'll be helping each other become better gardeners.

IRRIGATION

Irrigation is something that can break the bank—or it can be a cheap, simple addition to your watering routine. If spending thousands of dollars on an automatic watering system isn't in your budget, consider installing cheap drip hoses from your local hardware or home improvement store. You can manually turn these hoses on in one area while you're doing something else, such as harvesting, and complete two tasks at once! If drip irrigation isn't doable, you can always use a sprinkler.

When you're multitasking and irrigation is involved, always set a timer on your phone so you won't forget that the water is on. This is especially important with drip irrigation or soaker hoses, since it's not always easy to see if they're turned on if you're not close to them.

Weeding

This is the part of gardening that makes most people wrinkle their nose. Weeding should be part of your daily routine, even if you don't completely weed everything. Weeding one section of the garden for ten minutes or so each day adds up over time and helps you to keep on top of the weeds. You have a wide range of options to make weeding easier, even ways to make it unnecessary. Weed fabric, deep mulch, companion planting, and cover crops (as discussed in chapter 6) can help.

Pest Control

Evaluate your garden daily by spot-checking for pest damage or eggs. Many pests lay their eggs on the underside of the leaves of their favorite plants; removing these before they hatch can have exponentially positive effects on your garden. Identifying and picking off damaging pests—especially in their egg or larval stages—every day can keep numbers down and prevent the need for pesticides.

→ A pesty harlequin beetle sunning on a broccoli leaf

↓ Sometimes the simplest methods are the best way to remove squash bug eggs. This is a great daily task that only takes a few moments but results in big benefits.

WEEKLY TASKS

Spend a little time each week on these tasks and it will reduce your workload over the long term. Keeping things in check on a weekly basis prevents bigger problems from arising. Perhaps you can spend an hour every Saturday morning or Tuesday evening completing these slightly more substantial to-dos.

WEED FABRIC

The choice to use weed fabric can be a divisive issue. Also known as weed barrier or landscape fabric, this material has many detractors because most commercial versions are made from petroleum derivatives and might contain microplastics. We weigh these concerns against the fact that globalization has led to more weeds in our area than can be reasonably controlled by hand in a garden the size of ours.

To meet our preservation goals, we've invested in high-quality weed fabric that can be lifted and reused year after year. When choosing a woven weed fabric, don't be tempted to go with the lowest price point. We always look for a fabric rated to last several years, such as one with a five-year warranty. We also look for one that is made from tear-, puncture-, and UV-resistant woven fabric. You can also talk with local farmers who use weed barriers about what works best in your area. The weed fabric we use was recommended by a local farmer who had been using the same one in his garden for over fifteen years. While it's been a multi-year investment, the benefits we've seen in our garden have made it worth the cost and effort.

Removing bugs and eggs from your plants is something the whole family can help with.

Involving the whole family encourages everyone when the tasks get tedious.

Pruning

Different plant varieties call for specific pruning techniques. Pruning each plant the right way can make a ton of difference in the health and production of your garden. Pruning a tomato plant correctly will increase yields, for example, and it can help the plants stay on their trellises more effectively. In addition, some vining plants need to be pruned to maximize plant health and harvests. Pruning is a task best done weekly, but each plant has different needs and preferences for their pruning regimen, and they will all produce differently based on how they are pruned. Entire gardening books are devoted to pruning technique, so we won't delve into specific ones here. Just remember that it's an important subject to comprehend: proper pruning can help your garden prosper.

In-Ground Garden Watering

Depending on your climate, soil composition, and the types of plants you have, you may need to establish a weekly, thorough watering schedule. This process can be expedited in the layout stage of planning your garden. Consider putting plants that have similar water needs in the same general area of the garden, bearing in mind the type of soil and sunlight in that area. This is something you can fine-tune and change every year as your needs change and as you learn the specific watering requirements of your garden and plants.

Pest Control

Many pest and fungus control options are sprayed weekly. As with most gardening methods, the specific needs of your garden will vary based on your climate, the level of pest pressure, and what plants you're growing.

Mowing or Weed Whacking

General maintenance of the yard or area around your preservation garden isn't just cosmetic. Keeping the area surrounding the garden clean can prevent grasses and weeds from going to seed and infiltrating your garden. It also helps reduce cover and habitat for garden pests such as rabbits.

MONTHLY TASKS

While you can take care of some of the long-term gardening tasks more regularly if you desire, it isn't critical to perform these monthly tasks more frequently. As you'll soon see, though, keeping these tasks on your radar will improve yields and lessen the need for daily chores like weeding and watering (thanks, mulch!).

Succession Planting

Develop a monthly plan for succession planting (see chapter 2) and put it on your calendar. This practice maximizes your space and yields, something we all want. Using a garden planning app or website can help simplify this process. Alternatively, you can check seed packets for planting and maturity dates and map out your own succession planting schedule on paper. While you're at it, you can log potential harvest dates for each succession crop; this will help remind you to watch for the arrival of harvest time.

Remove Diseased, Dead, and Finished Plants

Even if you don't have a succession plan for every area of your garden, removing plants once they've stopped producing keeps your garden tidy, plus it removes cover and food for pests, diseases, and plant predators like deer and groundhogs. Removing diseased plant foliage is also essential for preventing the spread of pathogens.

Turn Your Compost

If you don't already have a compost bin or pile, consider starting one. Since you'll be growing

Snap peas grow quickly and are a great candidate for succession planting.

plants that need to be cleaned out at least once a year—and most of them (nightshades excepted) can be composted—you should have a wealth of materials available to get your pile started. It's also great motivation to save your kitchen scraps and fall leaves. For quality compost, turn the pile monthly (or more often if you want finished compost faster). There's nothing that offers the same satisfaction as making your own clean compost!

Add Mulch If Needed

Throughout the growing season, using mulch will help with weed control and keep precious moisture in the soil where you need it most. New mulch can be added at any time, but you should check all areas on a monthly basis and top them off with fresh mulch as needed. Doing so will help lessen your weeding and watering chores.

As you can see, with proper planning and deliberate action, spending a little time working in the garden on a daily or weekly basis can help you avoid gardening days that are more extensive, dedicated, and overwhelming to bring things back under control.

Getting It All Done: Scheduling and Planning

One of the biggest obstacles to gardening is thinking you have to finish everything at once. Block-scheduling your garden time can help with this. Depending on your personality, it can be hard to go into the garden and not take care of everything that needs to be done. Remember, though: most of the essential tasks can be done over time, not all at once.

Make a list of tasks and set a schedule. For many gardeners looking to preserve their own food, one hour a day of gardening is doable. Set a timer if you need to pace yourself. Personally, we like to go out an hour before sunset and let the sun be our timer. As an alternative schedule, we go out first thing in the morning and let the sun heating up the garden (and us!) be the timer. Both morning and evening are great times to get watering done, pull a few weeds, and fill your harvest basket. In the spring, planting can sometimes take a bit more time, especially if your garden is large.

TAKE SMALL BITES

If you have a small garden, you may be able to complete the bulk of your spring planting in a day or a weekend. For our large garden, we have to split up our work: it takes two to four weeks to wrap up all of our spring planting. Prioritizing and planning ahead can help, and remember that you can't possibly plant everything in a single day or even a week.

If you have a small backyard garden, you probably think we're making too much of this. We thought the same thing when we started gardening. We had four raised beds in the backyard and, at that time, it would take us a weekend to clean out and plant the entire garden at most. Now, with 4,000 square feet (372 sq m) of garden space filled with 90 tomato plants, 500 bush beans, 20 to 30 cucumbers, and 150 pepper plants (not to mention lots of other vegetables), we need a significant amount of time to get our planting done. In the spring we're also completing other farm tasks.

You may have a full-time job or kids finishing up the school year. Planning can go a long way as you prepare for this busy time. While you're planting your summer garden, you'll likely also be harvesting from your spring garden. Cool-weather spring crops such as radishes, lettuce, kale, spinach, bok choy, and cabbage are often ready to harvest right around the time the summer plants are ready to go in the ground, making your to-do

Assigning a monetary value to your produce and preserved foods helps you to visualize how much money you can save.

list especially long. Spring rains can also complicate and extend planting time requirements. Raised beds and no-till gardens are more flexible when it comes to planting between spring rains. If you mechanically till your garden, you should wait for it to dry out a bit to either till or to work the soil; if you don't, it can become a muddy mess.

REMEMBER WHY

Remember that it's normal at any point in the season to feel overwhelmed by your garden. Growing a food preservation garden is more than just a hobby. From time to time, you might need to remind yourself of your "whys" for growing your own food.

Every gardener has their own reason (or reasons) for wanting to grow and preserve their own food. For some, the focus is on cost savings. You're saving money by not spending money on food, essentially trading your time for food. If you work a job, you're trading your time for money, and you likely spend a good deal of that money on food. So why not grow your own and save that money to spend elsewhere?

For other gardeners, it may be more about the quality of the food they grow and preserve at home. When you're gardening and preserving your own food, the time you spend for food that is higher quality is the tradeoff for what you could buy at the supermarket.

Other reasons for growing and preserving your own food are highlighted throughout this book, and there are plenty. Whatever your reasons are, when things get overwhelming, remember those "whys" to see you through the challenges.

Preparing for Preservation

You can also block-schedule your preservation efforts in the same way you do for your gardening tasks. After harvest, many crops can be frozen and then otherwise processed to be shelf stable later. Examples include produce like tomatoes, peppers, onions, apples and other fruits, and berries. Some veggies keep for a week or more, or even longer, in the refrigerator. Carrots, radishes, and beets keep well in the fridge for weeks or even months (but note that they need to be in airtight containers to maintain high humidity). But, for the love of flavor and texture, do *not* put your tomatoes in the refrigerator unless they are in the form of sauce or salsa. Daily harvests of zucchini, cucumbers, okra, and beans can be stored short-term in the fridge and then preserved using your method of choice on weekends or whenever time allows.

All of this is to say: consider the extra fridge and freezer space you'll need if you don't have time to manage daily preservation projects during the harvest season.

Lifelong Learning

Gardening means continually learning—even after twenty years we're still learning new best practices in our garden. There are always new challenges that come up or a different technique that can save time or increase yield. Reading and watching videos from other gardeners can be valuable, but getting your hands dirty and just doing it will yield more long-term experience and value. In addition, you'll be passing that knowledge on to your children and grandchildren, or

Your food preservation strategy can be as varied as you want it to be. It's limited only by the types of food you grow.

your friends and neighbors, who may watch what you're doing and become interested in your gardening efforts. There's nothing more rewarding than teaching others who were previously uninterested in gardening or food preservation and sparking a passion to start their own projects.

USE YOUR COMMUNITY

Find like-minded friends nearby and lean on them—and let them lean on you—for filling gaps and handling excess harvest.

If you get so many tomatoes that you're overwhelmed, then become frustrated by the beetles eating all your cucumbers, let your gardening neighbor know. Maybe they're having the opposite problem, and you can trade your excesses to help each other out. Even a small community of people can help each other achieve great results together.

Time to Get to Work

With the garden maintenance tips offered in this chapter, coupled with the techniques revealed in prior chapters, your homegrown produce will soon be rolling in. Now it's time to dive into the next subject: the food preservation methods themselves.

TOO HOT TO CAN

As mentioned throughout this book, we love canned tomato sauce and salsa. We make gallons and gallons of it every year, by the pint and the quart. The bad part about canning anything is that it generates a lot of heat. We typically use water-bath canning for these foods, which you'll learn more about in the next chapter; this requires boiling water on the stove for about an hour at a time. When the tomatoes are coming in (July through September for us), we're already running the air conditioner in the house just to keep it comfortable, so adding more heat by boiling water in the kitchen is not ideal. This is where freezing tomatoes for later processing has extra benefits. We have a large section in a deep freezer set up just for tomatoes. When they're ripe, the whole tomatoes go into gallon bags in the freezer; we process these into sauce over the winter when generating the extra heat is beneficial rather than taxing our air conditioner.

After a few rounds, you'll figure out what a full batch of each produce type looks like, and will be able to determine, as it comes into your house, when you have enough to preserve a batch.

When we say batch, it can mean a canner full, a bag full for the freezer, a dehydrator full, or a freeze-dryer full. We'll go into each of these food preservation techniques in the next chapter. For now remember that, while it may feel like a lot of guesswork when you start, over time you'll get a feel for the best methods and times to turn your fresh produce into shelf-stable food.

SEASONAL PRESERVATION METHODS

When anthropologists talk about early man, they point to gardening and food preservation as some of our ancestors' earliest milestones. The evolution from gathering berries to planting and cultivating took generations, and from there finding ways to preserve the food for more than just hand-to-mouth use was a natural progression.

For humans to grow in a large, concentrated population, they had to be able to settle down and thrive in one place, in climates where food didn't grow year-round (meat notwithstanding). Our ancestors had to develop ways to grow and preserve food on a regular, reliable basis. From the early days of agriculture to the rise of complex civilizations, humans have worked to develop crops and farming techniques to meet their needs. The transition from hunter-gatherer societies to settled agricultural communities marked one of the most significant steps in human history. This shift allowed people to take control of their food supply rather than rely on unpredictable wild resources.

As human societies began to rely more on agriculture, they also had to contend with the challenge of food preservation. Before modern refrigeration and storage methods, other methods of food preservation were crucial to ensure survival through lean months or during periods of environmental stress. Early humans employed a variety of primitive preservation techniques, many of which are still used today.

This chapter will present some of these primitive methods of food preservation, such as drying, salting, pickling, and fermentation, as well as more modern methods of refrigerating, freezing, canning, and freeze-drying.

Storing dried foods and medicinal herbs is practical, and it also makes for beautiful pieces of home decor!

DEHYDRATION

Dehydration is one of the oldest food preservation methods. There are many versatile ways to dry food, even without a dedicated dehydrator. Dehydration removes moisture. When applied as a long-term storage method, it removes the medium in which bacteria, molds, and yeast consume and thereby spoil food. This will be a recurring theme as we discuss preservation methods.

Drying food as a means of preservation has been used since prehistoric times. Using the heat of the sun was the earliest, most basic method for dehydrating foods. Modern dehydration using warm air was developed over 200 years ago; this is what allowed companies to sell commercially dehydrated foods. Retail products like beef jerky and fruit roll-ups are the most common dehydrated foods people think of, but there are countless other options.

DEHYDRATING AT HOME

The most common method of dehydrating food for home preservation uses an electric food dehydrator. There are several brands and styles of dehydrators on the market, operating on the same principle—blowing warm air across the food to gradually wick moisture out of the food. Most also have a thermostat that enables the user to set the temperature of the blowing air. These are key, as too much heat can damage foods or cause them to change color and lose their nutritional value. "Low and slow" is the best when it comes to dehydration: we're trying to remove moisture, not cook the food.

↑ Apple slices, before and after a round in the dehydrator

← Herb salt is easy to make, and a great way to use herbs throughout the year.

You can also use a drying rack, which can be especially helpful for drying herbs that lose quality, color, and flavor at high temperatures; other foods can be dried with this method as well. A drying rack can be as simple as sticks woven together with food placed on them, allowing a breeze to cross the food.

As mentioned above, the sun's heat can be effective for drying foods. If you use this more natural method, be aware that ambient humidity levels may work against you: it's difficult to dehydrate food when the surrounding air is packed with moisture.

DEHYDRATION INSTRUCTIONS

Here are quick, simple instructions for the most popular methods of home dehydration.

Sun-Drying

During hot summer months, when the temperature rises to close to 100°F (38°C) for several hours, you can use the sun to dry tomato slices, apples, and other foods. The downside to sun-drying is that it can attract insects. Use insect netting to cover your sun-drying set-up to help prevent insects, especially flies, ants, and birds, from finding your dehydrating food. Another method that uses the sun is to place the food on a cooling rack on top of a sheet pan and put the rack on your car's dashboard on a hot day. As we all know, the interior of a car gets much hotter than the outside temperature, so this method can be used as long as the sun is strong, effectively extending the season for sun-drying your food after the hottest months of the year. Be selective about the foods you use for sun-drying, as it can be too hot for certain foods, including herbs.

Air-Drying

Perhaps the most popular method for dying herbs is air-drying. Herbs are laid out on a flat surface or hung to air-dry in bundles. They can be hung from a ceiling, on a wall, or you can use a foldable clothes-drying rack. Using a portable fan keeps air circulating and speeds up drying time. Herbs maintain more of their flavor, color, and medicinal properties when they're dried at temperatures less than 100°F (38°C). We dry many of our herbs in our pantry by hanging bundles of herbs, such as basil and lavender, from the exposed beams. How long the process takes depends on the herb and the conditions in your home. Herbs are dry enough when you can crumble them easily between your fingers.

Oven Drying

Using your oven as a dehydrator works well for many foods, such as herbs, fruit leather, and fruits and vegetables. Some ovens aren't the best for drying herbs because their lowest temperature setting is too warm (often 170°F to 190°F [77°C to 88°C]). If your oven has a bread-proofing setting, or even just an oven light, this usually heats the interior to just over 100°F (38°C), perfect for drying herbs. For fruits and vegetables, a temperature around 140°F (60°C) is ideal. If your oven doesn't go that low, keep a close eye on your dehydrating foods so they don't burn or get too crispy. Leave the door cracked open if possible or open the door from time to time to allow the moisture to escape the oven. The time required to oven-dry depends on the moisture content of the food you are dehydrating.

Fruit leather can be made on the dash of your car during a hot summer day.

Microwave Drying

Like oven drying, excessive heat can be the downside of microwave drying. Herbs can lose their flavor when dried at higher temperatures. I only recommend microwave drying if you're in a hurry or your environment is excessively humid, and you can't use the other options listed above. Here in southern Missouri, our humidity is typically high during the growing season, but we have no issue with air-drying herbs.

Dehydrators

Using a dehydrator allows you to dehydrate foods year-round, indoors, under more controlled conditions. The best dehydrators, such as the commercially available Excalibur, have temperature settings. Other features include thermostats, timers, stainless-steel trays, and reusable tray liners for liquid or sticky foods.

How long and at what temperature you should dehydrate different foods using an electric dehydrator depends on many factors, including how thick the pieces are, the type of food you're drying, its natural moisture content, the relative humidity, and the desired dryness level. All commercial dehydrators come with a manual that contains average drying times and temperatures for different fruits and vegetables, typically along with a handful of recipes for preparations like fruit leather.

With all dehydrated foods, you should ensure that they are dry enough to prevent mold or spoilage. Foods that haven't been fully dried will often grow mold when packaged. To catch any issues before storing dehydrated produce, place the dried food loosely into a screw-top jar to allow movement and put it somewhere that you can watch it daily. Seal the jar and shake it every day or two for a week. Look for signs of the food sticking together or clumping, or any moisture on the inside of the jar. If you notice any of these signs, put the whole batch back in the dehydrator. If dehydrated food begins to mold, throw it out. Once a week has passed with none of these signs, you can store your dehydrated food in an airtight container.

↑ Freshly harvested parsley, basil, thyme, and rosemary drying from the beams inside our house

↓ Dehydrated apple slices stored in a plastic bag

SALTING

People have been salting food for thousands of years. This is an efficient way to remove moisture from foods—including meats—creating an environment that is inhospitable for bacteria to reproduce, which makes it ideal for foods that would otherwise spoil quickly.

The advent of salting foods helped early people travel further from home, trade food with neighboring villages and other regions or countries, and keep food available over lean winter months. It also led to salt being more valuable than gold for a large part of human history. In fact, in the Roman Empire, soldiers' pay was based on the cost of salt: they were given a "salary" (based on the Latin word for salt, *sal*) so they could buy the most important staple of the day.

HOW TO SALT FOOD

Let's first explain why we're spending time on the one preservation method you are least likely to use extensively. While salting food as a sole food preservation method has largely been replaced by more modern methods, the history and methodology of salting offers an essential foundation for nearly all other food preservation techniques.

Salt helps to preserve food by reducing its water content and disrupting microbial cells that could cause spoilage. It takes a lot of salt (around 10 percent in a solution) to prevent bacteria from growing. This was once a mainstay in canning (1 cup [300 g] salt combined with 7½ cups [2 L] water makes a 10 percent solution). Today, many foods are preserved with salt and a combination of other preservation methods, such as canning, dehydration, refrigeration, or acidity.

Herb salt is a great way to preserve herbs and use them every day. We even sell jars of it as a value-added product.

We cure our own bacon with salt and sugar (sugar is another preservative, though we won't discuss it here). When curing bacon, we can see part of the salting process taking place: the pork belly is rubbed down with a mixture of one part salt to three parts sugar, along with herbs and spices. As the meat sits in this mixture, the salt and sugar disappear in their solid form, replaced with a liquid as a result of osmosis: the liquid from the meat is brought out and the salt dissolves into a saltwater solution. By removing the liquid from the meat, it is essentially dehydrated (though only partially). Other methods for curing meat involve the straight use of salt, rendering the meat shelf stable and obviating the need for refrigeration.

WHAT HAPPENED TO SALT PRESERVATION?

Modern refrigeration and pressure canning have had a profound impact on the use of salting for food preservation. Once the primary method for storing meat, dairy, and produce, salting gave way to the convenience offered by refrigeration.

Pressure canning also revolutionized home food preservation by enabling the high-temperature processing of low-acid foods like meats, poultry, vegetables, and even stews without using salt. The high heat in a pressure canner destroys bacteria and prevents spoilage, allowing foods to be safely canned and stored at room temperature for long periods.

Many home canners have adopted lower-salt or salt-free canning methods for two reasons: pressure canning can safely preserve foods without salt, and the modern diet has shifted away from consuming large amounts of salt. While it still plays a role in flavoring and texture in canned products, it's less necessary as a preservative compared with days before refrigeration and pressure canning.

When it comes to preserving vegetables, there's overlap between salting and fermentation (which we'll talk about in the next section). The two main methods of salting vegetables are dry salting and brining (wet salting).

Dry Salting

In this method, vegetables are layered with salt, which is applied directly to the cut surfaces of the vegetables or mixed through the vegetable pieces. Typically, a layer of salt is sprinkled at the bottom of a container (often a ceramic or glass jar or a crock), followed by a layer of vegetables, then another layer of salt, and so on. The salt draws water out of the vegetables through osmosis and the vegetable cells release moisture, which mixes with the salt to form a brine. When dry salting, keep applying fresh salt until it stays dry and no more moisture is drawn out; this works well for long-term storage. The whole idea behind salting (or dry brining, in this case) is to achieve an equilibrium in the medium (the food) by removing moisture and replacing it with salt to the point that bad bacteria cannot survive. When the food stops releasing moisture, you've hit that level.

Brining (Wet Salting)

In this method, vegetables are immersed in a saltwater solution (a.k.a. brine). The brine usually contains a specific ratio of salt to water—commonly around 5 to 10 percent salt by weight. The vegetables are placed in a jar or container and the brine is poured over them. The salt in the brine extracts moisture from the vegetables, which helps preserve them. A weight is often placed on top of the vegetables to keep them fully submerged in the brine, preventing exposure to air, the cause of spoilage. Most of the time when using brining, the final goal is fermentation, but the salt plays a crucial role in the food safety process. In a wet brine, you'll keep the food in the brine until consumption, otherwise ambient moisture in the air will rehydrate and "de-salt" the food to the point where bacteria can take hold again.

Because of the way we use salt and refrigeration and canning in modern times, people prefer other methods of food preservation for most vegetables. The only vegetables we preserve with salt are herbs. By using salt to pull the moisture out of herbs, you can enhance the flavor of both the salt and the dried herbs.

After salting foods comes another method with a long history: fermentation. When salting foods, a 10 percent salt solution is a rule of thumb, while increasing that solution to 15 percent or higher basically sterilizes the food and makes it incapable of supporting bacterial growth. Conversely, staying below 10 percent allows beneficial bacteria to enter the environment. When this process is controlled, we enter the sphere of fermentation.

FERMENTATION

Rather than removing liquid and bacteria from the food, as with salting, fermentation promotes the growth of "good bacteria." While salt can still be used, it's not present with this method at a high enough concentration to kill all bacteria.

The amount of salt you use depends on how you plan on storing the food. Storing your fermented food at room temperature (above 50°F [10°C]) requires using a higher salt concentration (3 tablespoons [42.5 g] to 1 quart [946 ml] water). If you're going to refrigerate your fermented food, you need half the amount of salt. Consider purchasing cultures and fermentation kits as you get started; these will help you learn the basics. When in doubt, refrigerate your fermented foods.

The process of growing good bacteria in your food will result in offgassing. The key to proper fermentation is to let the gasses escape your container without letting in ambient air that could come into contact with the food. While you can ferment foods using jars you already have, if you plan to do a lot of fermentation, a fermentation kit or a crock can be helpful. A fermentation crock has a water-filled lip and a fitted lid that creates a seal to let air escape but not enter. If you're going to make large batches of fermented food like kimchi or sauerkraut, you may want to invest in a fermentation crock.

A fermentation kit includes silicone fermentation lids for screw-top canning jars. You can also purchase fermentation weights, which are glass weights that hold the food in the brine to keep mold from forming. Some people use a baby food jar or something similar as a weight and cover their jars with cloth and a rubber band to hold the jar down in place. You can also use a normal canning jar lid and release the gasses by burping the jar daily.

Benefits of Fermentation

Fermented foods have been enjoyed for centuries, yogurt being the most familiar example. When you culture a food, you are increasing its shelf life by introducing beneficial bacteria. Since the human digestive system uses bacteria to break down foods within our bodies, ingesting some bacteria can be incredibly healthy. The opposite is also true: eating the wrong bacteria can be dangerous.

Kimchi and pickles are some of our favorite fermented foods. Kimchi has been eaten in Korea for thousands of years. The root of the word *kimchi* roughly translates to "submerged vegetables." While cabbage kimchi is most often served in Korean restaurants in the Western Hemisphere, most vegetables can be fermented using this process, with cabbage, cucumbers, and radishes being our favorites.

MAKING APPLE CIDER VINEGAR

Apple peels and cores aren't waste—use them to make your own apple cider vinegar via the process of fermentation.

Apple cider vinegar is easy to make, and so much better than what you buy in the store.

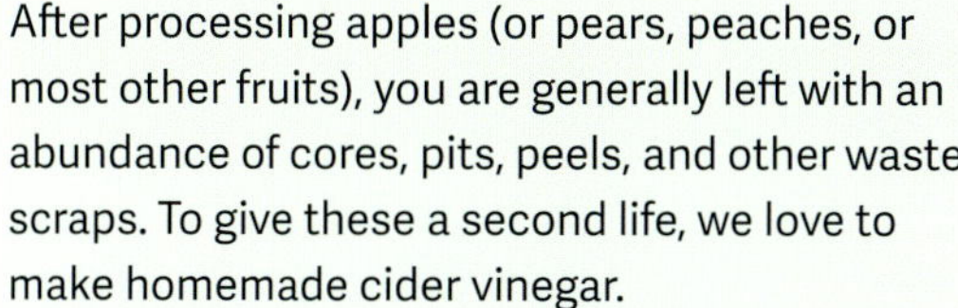

After processing apples (or pears, peaches, or most other fruits), you are generally left with an abundance of cores, pits, peels, and other waste scraps. To give these a second life, we love to make homemade cider vinegar.

To make your own apple cider vinegar (ACV), fill a half-gallon (1.9 L) canning jar three-quarters full of whole scraps. If you cut the pieces into smaller chunks, then just fill it half full. You can use all parts of the fruit. Add 2 tablespoons (30 ml) of "starter" apple cider vinegar—make sure you're using a natural vinegar that contains a mother, not a distilled vinegar. Next, add water. Fill the jar with a solution consisting of a ratio of 1 tablespoon (14 g) of sugar or honey per 1 cup (237 ml) of filtered, non-chlorinated water.

Cover with a fermentation lid or a tight-fitting cloth that will block bugs but allow air out (note that cheesecloth isn't a barrier for fruit flies). Let the mixture sit in a warm (65°F to 75°F [18°C to 24°C]), dark area for two weeks, stirring once a day. This keeps the sugar from settling, and it helps discourage bad mold from developing. We keep the jar on a shelf in our pantry with a towel over it to keep the light out.

After doing this for two weeks, strain the apples and sediment and decant the vinegar into a crock or a clean jar with a fermentation lid. Set in a dark area and leave it untouched for at least two months. At this point, the liquid should smell and taste like ACV and have a pH between 2 and 3. Make sure to reserve few tablespoons to start your next batch.

Most fermented vegetables will keep in cold storage (32°F to 50°F [0°C to 10°C]) for six to twelve months. Other fermented foods should be consumed or frozen after a few weeks to a month due to their alcohol content. This alcohol develops in high-sugar foods and increases over time. While it won't hurt you, this isn't the desired end state of the garden fermentation process covered here.

That said, you can make fruit wine out of a variety of garden produce—even tomatoes. More popular are the traditional wines made from strawberries and blackberries.

SIMPLE KIMCHI

INGREDIENTS

6 to 8 pounds (3 to 4 kg) napa cabbage, quartered lengthwise, leaving the stem intact
2½ cups (750 g) sea salt
2 tablespoons (16 g) sweet rice flour
2 cups (473 ml) water
2 cups (240 g) gochugaru chili powder (you can also use dried chili pepper flakes that you grow)
¼ cup (60 ml) fish sauce
¼ cup (30 g) minced garlic
¼ cup (30 g) chopped chives (cut in lengths around 1 inch [2.5 cm])
1 tablespoon (6 g) minced ginger
3 tablespoons (40 g) raw sugar
1 small yellow or white onion, minced

Thoroughly rinse the cabbage, dry, and coat liberally with salt—using at least 2 cups (600 g). Make sure to get the salt into the folds of the cabbage quarters, covering as much surface area as possible.

Put the cabbage into a food-grade bucket with a weight on top (like a plate and a heavy can or jug of water) for six to eight hours, rotating or stirring a few times during the process.

Remove the cabbage from the salt water (the salt will have drawn out the moisture from the cabbage) and rinse the remaining salt off each cabbage piece. Rinse the cabbage thoroughly, or your kimchi will be too salty to eat! Place in a colander to drain thoroughly for at least an hour.

In a saucepan, boil the water and add the sweet rice flour, gently simmer for 10 minutes, move to a mixing bowl, and allow to cool.

To the flour mixture, add 1 tablespoon (19 g) salt, along with garlic, ginger, sugar, onion, and chili flakes. Mix well.

Lay the cabbage quarters (now floppy) onto a sheet pan in groups and apply a coating of your mixture to each one, getting it down inside the leaves.

Transfer into an airtight container (we like to use gallon glass jars) and leave on the counter at room temperature for at least twenty-four hours. You should see some fermentation occur as bubbles appear, and the color of the cabbage changes. Since fermentation results in the release of carbon dioxide bubbles, be sure that the air has a way to escape the container to avoid a potential explosion or carbonation of the finished product. Then move it to the refrigerator to rest for three to four days to develop a more consistent flavor.

Optional: Chop the larger pieces to make them easier to eat. Store in the refrigerator.

We love to freeze-dry our kimchi pieces, making a tangy, crispy kimchi chip.

FERMENTED PICKLES

Most people think of canned dill pickles, but try fermented ones—they're amazing, and healthy! Lower in sodium and high in probiotics, these pickles are a healthy snack with a tangy flavor. They typically last about six months in the refrigerator. Since the cucumbers aren't boiled through the process of canning, they stay crunchier and heartier.

→ Fermented pickles are crunchier, crispier, and healthier than the canned pickles you find in stores.

FREEZING

Freezing, and the more general concept of cold storage, is a process that humans have used to preserve foods for hundreds or even thousands of years. Like most other forms of preservation, freezing and cooling works by making the food and its environment less hospitable to damaging bacteria, mold, and yeast. Since these microorganisms thrive in temperatures between 40°F and 90°F (4.4°C to 32.2°C), keeping foods below those temperatures will increase their shelf life.

Freezing doesn't have to be the final goal of preserving. Freeze tomatoes until you have time to can them.

Most modern homes have a freezer as standard equipment. We've become so accustomed to refrigeration in the kitchen that we often forget what a marvel it is. Modern electric freezers can increase the usefulness of fresh vegetables by months or years. Freezing can be more effective for particular foods, depending on their moisture content.

When water freezes, it expands, and when that water is inside your food, those tiny pockets of moisture expand, damaging or destroying the cell walls. Preserved food is relatively stable because it doesn't offer an environment where bacteria can grow, but the food itself may be damaged beyond usefulness due to the preservation process. This is why thawed foods are often mushy and don't have the same shape as their fresh counterparts. Because of this, low-moisture foods tend to freeze better than high-moisture ones. Compare a frozen green bean to a frozen tomato: a green bean will be relatively intact when it thaws, whereas a thawed tomato will be an unusable mess.

To help retain a good texture and bright color, most vegetables are blanched prior to freezing. Blanching is the process of placing the cut vegetables into a pot of boiling water for a few minutes to seal in flavor and color, then putting them immediately into an ice-water-bath to stop them from cooking.

The amount of blanching time required is different for each vegetable and the thickness of its cut. In general, the time ranges from one to four minutes. After the ice water is drained, the vegetables are dried and packed into freezer-safe containers for storage up to a year (sometimes longer in vacuum-sealed packaging). You'll learn more about blanching requirements for different vegetable profiles in chapter 5.

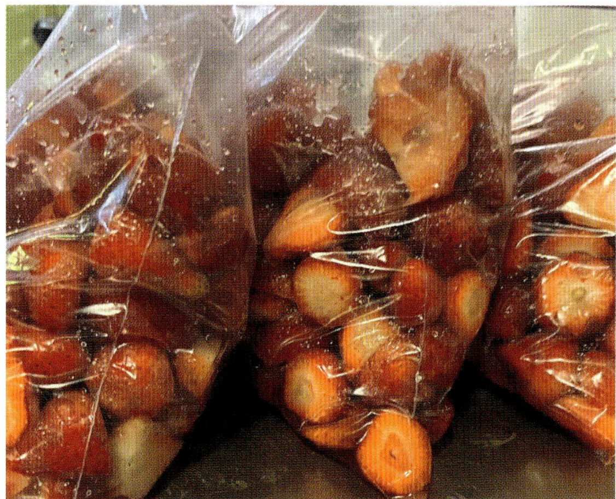

Strawberries are another food that can be frozen for later processing into jams or jellies.

COLD STORAGE METHODS

Today, we think of cold storage as the equivalent of a refrigerator, but electric refrigerators weren't seen in homes until the twentieth century. When they were first introduced, early refrigerators were simply an insulated box with ice inside to keep the food cold—an icebox—what we would think of today as a cooler. This method of cold storage became popular by the end of the 1800s and remained common until the 1930s.

The first electric refrigerator was developed in 1914, though this format didn't take off at first because it was too expensive for the average household. General Electric developed a more affordable electric refrigerator that was widely available in the late 1920s. The electric freezer was added as part of a refrigerator unit in 1930, followed by the development and widespread use of electric deep freezers in the 1940s. The

Using a vacuum sealer will keep vegetables like these potatoes from getting freezer burn and can greatly extend their freezer life.

increased use of deep freezers was partly due the need for large-scale food preservation during World War II, when the military and food industries began to rely heavily on freezing technology. Manufacturers soon adapted these methods for household use.

The icebox, and then the refrigerator, changed how modern people ate and how they stored food. In many ways, these developments spelled the beginning of the end for other traditional food preservation methods. It is now much more common in the twenty-first century to keep perishable foods refrigerated or frozen than it is to use any shelf-stable preservation methods. In the mid-1930s, New Deal loans led even more Americans to switch to electric refrigerators. The history of refrigerators and cold storage—and how they radically transformed other traditional food preservation methods in the twentieth century—isn't widely known, but this technology changed the way people buy, store, and consume their food.

The Root Cellar

The original cold storage began underground, in a root cellar. When you dig into the ground, the temperature is cooler in the summer and warmer in the winter, making it generally stable year-round. How cool it will stay depends on where you live and how deeply you dig. Most old root cellars were dug out and then had a building or door placed over the top to help keep the cold air inside. To further help maintain cool temperatures, these pits would be lined with stone, with ice sometimes stored there for better cooling.

Storing food in root cellars has as much to do with humidity as it does with temperature. The ideal storage temperature for a root cellar is 32°F to 40°F (0°C to 4.4°C)—similar to what is standard for our modern-day refrigerators. Where the two differ is in the humidity of the cooling space. Modern refrigerators often don't provide much humidity, whereas root cellars are typically very humid. This supports storing vegetables that prefer higher humidity, keeping them from drying out. There are some veggies that prefer low humidity and slightly higher temperatures, such as onions, garlic, and sweet potatoes. Produce like this benefits from storage in a dry cellar with temperatures closer to 40°F to 55°F (4.4°C to 12.8°C) and humidity below 80 percent.

Cold storage in the form of freezing and root cellars, as well as refrigeration, will be discussed in more depth in the produce profiles section in chapter 5. There we'll cover how to cold store or freeze each specific vegetable profiled.

ICE HARVESTING

Ice harvesting was common in America in the early 1800s. Ice was cut from ponds, lakes, and rivers into blocks, then transported and stored underground and sold to people who needed it to help keep their food cold.

CONTAINER CHANGE

It's interesting to note how containers for stored food have changed over the years. Before refrigerators, most families owned heavy stoneware crocks of different sizes to keep in their houses and cellars. With the advent of ice boxes and refrigerators, we've moved to a standard of small, lightweight, stackable containers that hold smaller amounts of food.

WATER-BATH CANNING

Home canning and industrial canning have a shared history. Yet, while their origins are linked, the two methods are very different. To stay true to the theme of this book, we'll focus on home canning here.

Like so many developments in our modern world, the development of canning started with the necessities of war. An effort to improve and standardize the nutrition of soldiers eventually led to finding the best ways to can food.

In the 1870s, soon after the American Civil War, home canning as we recognize it today really took off. John Landis Mason invented the metal screw-top Mason jar in 1858 in the United States, and the first Ball jars were manufactured and widely distributed starting in 1884.

Tin cans and glass jars are also part of the history of canning. Glass is easier for a home canner to use, and the containers can be reused indefinitely—we have Ball jars in our pantry that are well over one hundred years old that we still can in, always using new lids and rims. But, as glass has an irregular stacking shape and weight, making it difficult to transport as part of an army's rations, tin cans became optimal for shipping over long distances.

WHEN IT STARTED

Near the end of the eighteenth century, Napoleon Bonaparte recognized that his army was subsisting almost completely on salted pork. He knew this wasn't sustainable, so he declared a competition for the development of a method to improve nutrition for his troops.

The first forms of canning (what we would today call oven canning) came about fifteen years later. In 1809, French chef Nicolas François Appert used a cork to seal jars that had been heated in an oven. According to the United States Food and Drug Administration (FDA), this method is not considered safe for preserving food; nevertheless, in its general form this method is still widely used throughout the world.

Over the next one hundred years, canning developed to where it is today, with the general idea being that heated contents of a jar will shrink when cooled. If a seal is introduced while the jar is heated, it will create an airtight vacuum once the product cools. In the process, the heating of the jars and their contents kills all bacteria, and no new bacteria can enter the sealed container. While this was adopted effectively in the early 1800s, *why* it worked was not fully understood until Louis Pasteur discovered the principles of pasteurization in 1863.

Around the time of the Great Depression, beginning in the 1920s, the United States

Department of Agriculture (USDA) began issuing guidelines for home canning and statements about safe and unsafe canning practices. Over the years, these guidelines have grown: today, many people are so overwhelmed and scared that they avoid any kind of home canning, considering all of it dangerous.

CANNING ACIDIC VERSUS NON-ACIDIC FOODS

When acidity comes up in conversations about canning, eyes glaze over and people decide canning is too hard.

Since the topic of this book is gardening for the purpose of food preservation, we're not going to give detailed instructions on the intricacies of canning. It's still important to have some general guidelines so that you know when to water-bath foods and when you need to pressure-can.

As a general rule, if the food is acidic (with a pH lower than 4.6), it can be water-bathed canned. If it is low acid (with a pH higher than 4.7), it should be pressure canned. Durations of both vary by the food and the size of jar you are using, but the general idea is that canning under pressure yields a higher temperature than just water-bath canning (around 240°F [115.6°C]). This is deemed necessary when the acidity of the food cannot be counted on to prevent spoilage.

Out of an abundance of caution, it is often recommended to add additional acid to acidic foods like tomato products. When it comes to foods that

Canning many foods takes labor to change them into the final product. Make it a fun activity for the kids and they'll want to help.

But What About Botulism?

Botulism is a serious illness caused by the toxins created by *Clostridium botulinum* bacteria. It's a real problem and should be taken seriously—but it should not be feared to the point that you avoid canning altogether. When you know how it can be prevented, and how to carefully plan canning techniques using tested recipes, botulism should be no scarier than anything else in life. Botulism is unique in the world of food-harming microorganisms in that, unlike most bacteria, it thrives in a low-oxygen and low-acid environment. People are often afraid because botulism has no smell or taste. If you're afraid or in doubt, though, boil preserved food for ten to twenty minutes after opening a jar: this will destroy the botulism spores.

FORJARS

are *usually* acidic enough, there's some evidence that their levels vary too much for safe canning. Adding a small amount of lemon juice or citric acid as called for by a recipe removes any doubt in the process. Many recipes for canning high-acid foods such as peaches, apples, blackberries, and grapes also call for adding acid at the time of canning, just for safety's sake. We use a home pH meter to determine if foods are acidic enough for safe water-bath canning. Taking this extra step gives us peace of mind when we want to skip the added acid or if we want to develop our own recipes.

↑ We use our pressure canner as a water-bath canner for acidic foods like tomato sauce—by leaving the lid off.

← Water-bath canned peaches are a staple in our house.

STORING CANNED FOODS

One great thing about canned food products is that they're shelf stable in places throughout your home. They don't require refrigeration or even cool storage in a basement or a cellar. General ambient room temperatures are fine for properly canned foods. The only factors to consider are sunlight and temperature: temperatures over 80°F (27°C), as well as bright light directly hitting the food, will likely cause color changes, changes in nutritional value, and, in theory, could affect flavor.

At a minimum, it will make the food look less desirable. In our experience, the food will still be safe and taste okay, but a brown pint of strawberry preserves is not the most appetizing topping for your PB&J! Some foods, like strawberries, are much more sensitive to color changes due to room temperature and sunlight. Always remember to look over your canned foods as a whole and smell each jar before using the contents. If one jar is a different color than the rest, or if it smells off, or the lid wasn't sealed as tightly as the others, these may be indicators of spoilage.

PRESSURE CANNING

Pressure canning is an extension of the prior section about water-bath canning, as the methods are similar in theory and in application. We've already outlined many of the differentiators between both methods and discussed which foods should be preserved using pressure canning, so this section will be considerably shorter than the last.

Pressure cooking has been around since the 1600s, when people realized that cooking foods under pressure allows the temperature to get as high as 240°F (116°C) and makes foods cook faster and more thoroughly. Bone broth, soups, and stews could be cooked in a fraction of the time, saving precious fuel and time.

It was only a matter of time before the concept of water-bath canning would be combined with pressure cooking to enable humans to can foods faster and at a higher temperature. Pressure canning became popular in the early 1900s with Presto's introduction of a home pressure canner.

WHICH FOODS TO PRESSURE CAN

As mentioned in the previous section, low-acid foods should be pressure canned instead of water-bath canned. Also, any type of meat should be pressure canned. We use our pressure canner for broths, soups, and chili, as well as for green beans, potatoes, corn, and dry beans. It's great to have ready-to-use black beans sitting right on the shelf.

CANNED FOOD IS TOO SALTY

Home canners often hear complaints from people who don't preserve their own food: canned food is too salty. This stems from the days when salt was used as a preservative. Such high salt levels aren't necessary for preserving most foods these days, so modern canned foods shouldn't be salty. The stereotype of canned food being salty isn't really true anymore, but it's still a bias that may take generations to overcome.

Many prepared and mass-produced foods today *are* made with additional salt so that they'll be more appetizing. Salt releases dopamine, making people crave it, which is one reason why fast food is so addictive. Most foods that are pressure canned can be safely prepared at home with minimal or no additional salt.

↑ We use pressure-canned potatoes most often in our meals.

→ Canned green beans are often associated with being salty, but with modern home pressure canning, they don't have to be.

FREEZE-DRYING

The technology used to make home freeze-drying possible has gone mainstream. We liken it to the advent of electric refrigerators or even microwave ovens: when the technology was new, it was expensive and untrusted.

Once the market drives down the price and freeze-drying becomes both affordable and normalized, everyone will have one of these appliances. Can you imagine not having a refrigerator in your house? We believe there will be a time in the not-so-distant future when home freeze-dryers will be as common as refrigerators and microwave ovens.

Like so many great culinary discoveries, the French get credit for inventing freeze-drying. In 1906, Jacques-Arsène d'Arsonval of the Collège de France in Paris developed the theories and concepts behind freeze-drying.

Before it was widely used for food, freeze-drying was employed during World War II for preserving and transporting blood serum. The key benefit of this technique over others was recognized early: unlike drying or curing, you don't have to use salt and, unlike canning methods, you don't have to use extreme heat. Both are damaging to the vital nutrients of food, and even more damaging to biological materials.

Freeze-dried strawberries are some of our family's favorite snacks.

It wasn't until after the war that the commercial freeze-drying of foodstuffs took off. In the past decade, home freeze-drying has become a reality, and more commonplace as the cost barrier to entry has dropped substantially.

HOW FREEZE-DRYING WORKS

The technical term for freeze-drying is lyophilization, which is probably why the term "freeze-drying" is more widely used.

Though the technology is relatively new, the reasoning behind freeze-drying is one that the ancient Egyptians would understand. The purpose is to remove all moisture from the food, making it difficult or impossible for bacteria to enter the food to spoil it.

This is done through a three-step process.

Freezing

While the process of freezing sounds simple, it's the crucial step in achieving the best final product. When a food freezes, the water molecules expand. If you've ever exploded a liquid container in your freezer, you're familiar with this phenomenon. Let's use an apple slice as an example:

One of our favorite things about freeze-drying is that you can preserve different foods in mixed loads.

When you freeze the fruit and then thaw it, the result is a mushy apple slice. This is because the cell walls of the apple slice become damaged when the water inside them freezes and expands. When thawed, the ice no longer holds the structure together and the cell structure is left in a damaged state.

This means that, the more rapidly a food freezes, the less damage to the solid structure of the food. Commercially made freeze-dryers refrigerate the chamber as quickly as possible for this purpose.

Sublimation Drying

After the contents of the freeze-dryer (in this example, apple slices) are frozen, air pressure is reduced by a vacuum pump attached to the machine. Once the majority of the air is removed, the temperature is slowly raised back above freezing to a point specified by the user, usually programmed into the machine. As the ice melts, it sublimates, transiting to a gaseous state. At this point, approximately 95 percent of the moisture is removed from the apple slices, and the moisture takes the form of a gas within the chamber.

Desorption Drying

The process is repeated to remove the remaining moisture from the chamber, and the gaseous moisture inside the chamber becomes solid ice on the outside, leaving the dried food in the center. In the case of a home freeze-dryer full of apple slices, the layer of ice around the outside of the chamber will be as much as 1 inch (2.5 cm) thick. Foods with a lower moisture content, such as green beans, will produce less moisture.

WHAT CAN'T I FREEZE-DRY?

Freeze-drying only removes water from foods. This means that fatty or extremely sugary foods such as foods rich in butter or honey should not be freeze-dried. Sugary foods tend to expand (or, in some cases, explode) in the freeze-dryer, leaving a mess, or a perfectly crunchy, fluffy version of your favorite candy. Nearly all the garden produce we've tried in our freeze-dryer has been a success. Just remember three things do not freeze-dry: chocolate, honey, and oil.

RECONSTITUTION AND USE

Once you have a freeze-dried apple slice (or green beans or a slice of zucchini or whatever produce), you don't just add water and have the original specimen on your plate. Regardless of how fast step one in the freeze-drying process goes, there will be some damage to the structure of your food. That's not all bad, though: the damage is comparable to what happens when you freeze foods in the traditional way. Most people are familiar with the floppy texture of a frozen and thawed green bean or piece of zucchini.

↑ Squash is easy and fun to process as a freeze-dried food.

→ Freeze-dried squash is one of our favorite foods.

↓ Snap peas, squash, and green beans being reconstituted in quart (946 ml) jars

When you freeze-dry produce in its most natural state, you'll be able to add water and use it in your recipe, and often you can't even tell that it was preserved. Foods like green beans and zucchini are some of our favorites to freeze-dry. As with freezing, you preserve more of the nutritional value with freeze-drying, which preserves the most nutrients of any shelf-stable food preservation method. In our experience it also preserves the truest flavor of the foods.

We choose not to reconstitute many of the foods we freeze-dry—we just enjoy them crunchy. Freeze-dried strawberries, apple slices, peach slices, and carrot sticks are some of our favorite snacks. As a bonus, since the freeze-drying process removes only water, all of the flavor remains and becomes extra concentrated. That apple slice will be crunchy and super-flavorful! This can make these foods appealing to a wider audience, making it easier for a family to switch to healthier, one-ingredient options by essentially producing a whole range of snack foods. When considering freeze-drying, think beyond the constraints of just preserving food: consider the ways freeze-drying can unlock new ways to enjoy your foods.

And freeze-drying isn't just for raw, core ingredients out of the garden. Prepared foods, such as casseroles, stews, and scrambled eggs, are great freeze-dried, as they are easily reconstituted and are now shelf stable. We also love to freeze-dry unconventional snacks like kimchi, making a crunchy chip that's healthy and fun to eat. When working with foods like kimchi, the settings on the freeze-dryer can be adjusted to limit the heat applied to the food while it's drying, allowing you to dry foods at a temperature that will not harm beneficial probiotics.

STORING FREEZE-DRIED FOOD

Once the food comes out of the freeze-dryer, it has to be stored somewhere. Two things we love about freeze-dried foods: they have a superlong shelf life (up to twenty-five years) depending on how you store them, and your storage options are vast.

For short-term storage (one to two years), we use glass canning jars—the same jars we use for canning. We have several antique Ball and Kerr jars dating back to the early 1900s that we don't use for traditional water-bath or pressure canning because they're more likely to break, but we will still use them to store freeze-dried foods. Depending on how quickly we plan to eat the food, we generally use pint (473 ml) and quart (946 ml) jars. This comes from years of canning a large amount of food for our family: we have a huge collection of glass jars and also a pantry where we can store them.

If you're new to food storage, you may be able to set up a different system that allows for more affordable storage. Mylar bags are one option: We use these for longer-term storage (for between two and twenty-five years). Whatever you decide, be sure to get a disposable oxygen absorber. The two main enemies to freeze-dried food are moisture and oxygen, so a tight seal and an oxygen absorber give you the keys to success. Mylar and glass are both materials that won't let any oxygen or moisture into the container.

Canning Jars

Storing freeze-dried food in canning jars isn't the most space-efficient method for storage, but it offers many benefits. For one thing, since jars are see-through, they're a great way for the family to pick what they want for a snack. Our kids love to go into the pantry and grab a jar of freeze-dried strawberries or bananas when they feel hungry for something light. Even a jar of freeze-dried baby carrots are a favorite, dipped in hummus.

Canning jars are also reusable, so your cost-per-preservation cycle is pennies—really, it's just the cost of the oxygen absorber, since the lid flats can be reused for storing freeze-dried foods, unlike in traditional canning where you have to purchase new flat lids every time. If you plan to eat your foods in a few months and you want to avoid using oxygen absorbers, you can use a jar vacuum sealer to seal the jars.

Canning jars are great for reconstituting freeze-dried foods, too, because you can just pop the lid and add water (boiling, hot, or cold tap water, depending on the food).

Remember that canning jars let in light, which is their main drawback. Depending on your storage location, this can cause foods to lose color and nutrients. We've found that foods high in beta-carotene, such as carrots and sweet potatoes, tend to lose their color and turn white soon after we store them. They still taste fine, but don't look particularly appetizing.

While not necessary for all foods, a jar vacuum sealer can be used remove air from your Mason jars and *may* increase the preserved foods' shelf life.

Mylar Bags

As mentioned above, we use Mylar bags for long-term food storage of freeze-dried foods. They keep moisture and light out and can be a space-efficient option. If you have limited storage space, you could even store a bin of Mylar bags of food under your bed in case of emergency.

Storing in Mylar has some downsides. Curious mice sometimes eat holes in the bags to see what's inside. We've lost quite a few bags that way. Our solution is to store Mylar bags of long-term foods inside mouse-proof storage bins.

The other point to consider is the cost of Mylar bags. While they can be washed and reused, they require an impulse sealer to close them. Every time you open one, you lose some of the bag's length, which means that eventually it will be unusable. Also, unlike canning jars, you don't have the option to skip oxygen absorbers when you seal Mylar bags.

Other Storage Options

Many people use sealable plastic buckets. Lidded buckets can be convenient because they're easily resealable, reusable, and very versatile, as a bucket can be used in countless ways.

While we don't use buckets for our long-term storage of freeze-dried foods—and we're not against them in principle—we prefer to keep our long-term foods in rectangular, serving-sized containers, which maximize storage space and allow us to access just the right amount of food we need.

← Tomatoes are fun to eat in their freeze-dried state—they're like tomato-flavored croutons for your salad.

Seasonal Food Preservation Tasks

Food preservation looks different for everyone, depending on how many people you're feeding, your food preferences, how you eat your food, and your food preservation goals.

Each season has tasks to complete that will help you meet your goals, and each is as important as the next. It's easy to focus on harvesting and canning (for example), but you need a clear plan to back up these steps, and a commitment to do the work over the year.

Use winter to plan and get organized. Most people don't give food preservation much thought over the winter, except when they're eating their harvest from the previous season. In reality, winter is the best time to work out your plan and prepare for success.

If you haven't decided how much you're going to preserve and how you're going to do it until planting season is upon you, you're committing yourself without the foresight you need to be successful. Also remember that you won't be alone if you wait until it's time to start your garden, so you'll be competing with other people for supplies and equipment. Sometimes you can get better deals ordering and purchasing things in the off-season.

INVENTORY AND PLANNING

It doesn't matter when you do begin planning, but try to have a dedicated time each year when you focus on this step. We like to make our plans in the winter, but you can do it when it fits your schedule and lifestyle. Just don't skip it! A simple planning process will be crucial for setting and achieving your goals.

Take inventory of all the canned goods, dehydrated foods, freeze-dried foods, and anything in your freezers. Make an honest assessment of what you've used so far in the season, what you have left on hand, and what you're likely to need for next season.

Questions to Ask Yourself as You Plan

- What are you likely to run out of?
- Do you want to preserve more of something next season?
- Do you have enough of something, so you won't have to preserve any next year?
- Did you not eat as much of something as you had expected in the last season? Should you take it out of your preservation lineup?
- What did you not have this year that you want to add next year?

Once you've answered these questions, you should have a good idea of what to grow next year—or at least source elsewhere—for home preservation. We find that winter is the best season to think through these questions.

Ordering Equipment and Supplies

As mentioned in the last section, we like to plan and order our supplies in the winter rather than waiting until everyone else is ordering their annual supplies. People tend to order their seeds in the spring, just when planting should begin. Most seed companies have their seeds packaged and ready for sale early in the winter, before the growing season, so you'll have a better selection—especially when it comes to hot new items—if you order before the crowds do.

Other Items to Inventory and Order

- Purchase garden supplies, such as weed fabric, trellising, and fencing
- Order canning equipment and supplies you should replace regularly, such as jars, lids, pectin, and citric acid
- Check the seals on your canner for damage, wear, and need for potential replacement
- Stock up on oil for your freeze-dryer

- Inventory and buy seeds
- Create or update your own preserving and gardening goals

Your garden may not be growing in the winter (or it might be, depending on your climate), but you can still use this time for food preservation to make the most of your overall seasonal food storage.

Take time in the winter months to preserve whatever isn't keeping as long as you had hoped in your root cellar or cold storage.

↑ We always stock up on freeze-dried kale that we use for powder in the spring.

↗ Fresh cabbage

→ Processing corn isn't hard, but it can be tedious.

← Empty your freezer and can what may need a format change during winter—this takes advantage of the heat produced by the canning process to warm your living space.

PRESERVATION BY SEASON

This list will give you some ideas of foods to preserve and preservation methods to use based on when they are in season. Your results may vary based on your climate, growing season, and even your preferences. These items are based on what we typically preserve by season but, of course, your climate and growing season might change the placement of some of these items.

Winter Preservation

PRESSURE CAN

- ☐ Vegetable broth from scrap vegetables collected in the freezer
- ☐ Potatoes
- ☐ Winter squash cubes
- ☐ Sweet potatoes

WATER-BATH CAN

- ☐ Picked onions
- ☐ Cranberry sauce, cranberry jelly

DEHYDRATE OR FREEZE-DRY

- ☐ Onions
- ☐ Celery
- ☐ Garlic

NOTE: We do our catch-up canning in winter. There are a few reasons why we need to focus our attention on making up for what we couldn't get to before. We might have run out of time to finish everything during harvest season, or maybe we put it off until colder weather came. We often preserve items from fresh storage because they haven't lasted as long as we'd hoped.

For instance, sometimes it's more efficient to throw a bunch of ripe tomatoes directly into the freezer in the summer and can them in the winter. The process of cooking down sauce and water-bathing the jars generates heat and humidity that wouldn't be comfortable in August, but it sure is welcome in January.

Spring Preservation

FREEZE

- ☐ Asparagus
- ☐ Strawberries
- ☐ Spinach
- ☐ Peas (sugar snap, shelling, snow)
- ☐ Broccoli

WATER-BATH CAN

- ☐ Cabbage (sauerkraut)
- ☐ Strawberry jam
- ☐ Strawberry pie filling

PRESSURE CAN

- ☐ Asparagus

DEHYDRATE

- ☐ Kale (or spinach)
- ☐ Strawberries (sliced, or fruit leather)

FREEZE-DRY

- ☐ Asparagus
- ☐ Peas
- ☐ Strawberries
- ☐ Broccoli
- ☐ Cauliflower
- ☐ Cabbage (kimchi chips)
- ☐ Kale

Summer Preservation

FREEZE

- Corn
- Green beans
- Berries
- Shredded or diced zucchini/squash
- Diced onions and peppers

WATER-BATH CAN

- Pickled peppers
- Cucumbers, pickled and relish
- Peaches
- Jams and jellies
- Berry pie fillings

PRESSURE CAN

- Corn
- Potatoes
- Green beans

DEHYDRATE

- Fruit leather
- Herbs (oregano, basil, dill, thyme, parsley, etc.)
- Onions

NOTE: Instead of drying onions in a plastic dehydrator (which will smell like onions forever after), consider investing in stainless-steel trays or buying dedicated onion trays.

FREEZE-DRY

- Corn
- Green beans
- Berries
- Shredded or diced zucchini/squash
- Diced onions and peppers
- Tomatoes (sliced, diced, sauce)
- Herbs

Fall Preservation

FREEZE

- Pumpkin purée and other winter squash

WATER-BATH CAN

- Apples (sauce, pie filling, juice)
- Plums
- Pears (butter or sliced/diced)
- More tomatoes
- Pickled peppers

PRESSURE CAN

- Green beans

DEHYDRATE

- Apple/Peach/Pear slices
- Fruit leather
- Peppers
- Fruit slices
- Peppers
- Tomatoes
- Green beans
- Sweet potatoes
- Winter squash purée (into powder for easy baking)

Bonus: Food Preservation for Easy Meal Prep or Snacks

WATER-BATH CAN

- Fruits for side dishes (peaches are a favorite in our house)
- Pasta sauce
- Ketchup
- Salsa

PRESSURE CAN

- Dry beans (which turn into canned beans)
- Stews, pot roast, chili
- Ready to use ingredients: potatoes, carrots
- Beans
- Corn

DEHYDRATE

- Dehydrated fruit
- Fruit leather

FREEZE-DRY

- Soups, casseroles, and lasagna
- Cooked meats, such as ground beef and chicken breasts

↑ Pressure canned soup or chili is a quick meal anytime.

→ Be careful dehydrating spicy peppers: consider moving your dehydrator outside to avoid making your kitchen uninhabitable for days. Ask us how we know.

PRODUCE PROFILES

In this chapter, we profile our favorite foods to grow for preservation. A comprehensive list of foods you can grow and preserve would be too large for any book. We won't cover every food we could possibly grow or every kind of food we could preserve here–the idea is to paint a picture of growing one version of the ideal preservation garden. We'll showcase some of the foods we think people might enjoy growing in their preservation garden, either because they like the food or because it might be something new (but not too radical) to broaden their horizons.

TOMATOES

Tomato plants can be huge, but training them to grow up makes them an efficient producer.

DETERMINATE VERSUS INDETERMINATE

Determinate tomatoes set all of their fruit at once, while indeterminate tomatoes make new foliage, flowers, and fruit throughout the growing season until they're killed by frost.

NOTE: We've said it before and will say it again: we love tomatoes. What follows is an extensive dive into the subject, longer and more in-depth than the other produce profiles that follow.

Tomatoes can be grown in *many* different ways. Some plants are bigger than others—some grow like bushes, while others are vine-like. In general, indeterminate tomatoes that are allowed to branch need about 3 feet (91 cm) of space to spread across a trellis. A tomato cage will *not* be

↑ Tomatoes are, by far, our favorite produce to grow.

← Guiding tomatoes through the cattle panel trellis

↘ Our tomatoes are picked when blushing, then ripen in the pantry.

enough support for most types of tomato plants. Many indeterminate tomatoes will grow over 8 feet (2.4 m) tall (long).

If left to their own devices and unsupported, they'll grow along the ground, which is not great for tomato production. When they grow this way it's nearly impossible to harvest tomatoes, plus they become vulnerable to many more types of pests, such as ants, voles, armyworms, and pillbugs (a.k.a. roly polys). Trellising tomatoes also saves space, much like other vertical growing methods. In addition, trellising protects the plants from soil-borne pathogens, prompts airflow around the plants, and helps reduce fungal disease.

There are a few things to consider when deciding how to trellis tomatoes: what type of tomato to grow, where you're growing it, and how much time and labor you can put into building and maintaining the trellis—and, to an extent, how many tomatoes you are growing.

We trellis our tomatoes on steel cattle panels. We attach the panels to T-posts about knee high off the ground (20 to 24 inches [51 to 61 cm]). The panels are 16 feet (4.9 m) long, and we have fifteen of them in our garden at this time with three to five tomato plants growing on each panel. This setup works best, giving us a flat surface where we can see all of the tomatoes growing and can easily prune and harvest them. We prune and guide the tomatoes through the cattle panel trellis about once a week—sometimes twice a week if they're growing quickly. With over ninety tomato plants per year, it takes us around an hour and a half to prune and trellis all our plants once a week. We stop pruning to save time when the plants begin producing lots of fruit. Things get a little messy late in the season, but production and efficiency are more important to us than having a pretty, neat, tidy garden.

Some other support methods, like tomato cages and the Florida weave (a.k.a. basket weave), are more suited to smaller determinate varieties like Roma types. Tomato cages will generally be outgrown by almost any indeterminate tomato plant. Some growers tie their tomatoes to fenceposts or stakes, or they trellis them with ropes hanging from a support system. This type of trellising is common when growing in high tunnels, and it works best in conjunction with heavy pruning to a single leader. The Florida weave is commonly used for determinate varieties grown in open fields or high tunnels—but it's not ideal if you need to prune your tomatoes. Like so many things, *the best method is the one that works for your goals.* High production from a lot of plants is our goal, so efficiency is the name of the game.

PLANNING CONSIDERATIONS: How many tomatoes you plant will depend not only on how many tomato products you want to preserve but on what types of tomatoes you're growing and how much space you have. We generally split tomato varieties into three categories: cherry, slicer, and sauce (though there are more variations, such as salad tomatoes and grape tomatoes).

While cherry tomatoes are high producers, they aren't the best for canning—instead they're better eaten fresh. (When they overwhelm us, we make sauce out of them). Remember that tomatoes are extremely versatile, and you can preserve any of them or enjoy any of them fresh.

SUN REQUIREMENT: Full sun. Fruits can be prone to sunburn in hot climates. If your tomatoes are in full sun and your peak temperature climbs above 95°F (35°C), you may need to create afternoon shade or use a shade cloth.

GROWING SEASON: Summer. Tomatoes are frost tender. Most tomato varieties need ninety to over one hundred days to mature from seed. If you have a shorter growing season, look for short-season varieties that mature in seventy to ninety days; some can be ready in as few as fifty days. We always plan to put our first succession of tomatoes in the ground as soon as we feel the threat of frost has passed, which is early May for us.

PESTS: Tomatoes are the target for many pests—they're so yummy! Squirrels, birds, aphids, stinkbugs, leaf-footed bugs, tomato hornworms, armyworms, cutworms, earwigs, and more all love tomatoes. While this list is in no way exhaustive, don't be discouraged: pest problems aren't a given when you grow tomatoes, and there are many ways to deal with pests if they do appear.

HARVESTING: It may be shocking, or something you've already heard, but you don't need to let your tomatoes ripen on the vine for amazing homegrown flavor. To maximize yields and crop quality, we harvest our tomatoes when they begin to blush. Everyone loves ripe tomatoes, so if you leave the fruits on the plants to fully ripen, someone or something may find them first. This mainly applies to slicers and sauce tomatoes, but it works for cherry tomatoes as well. Harvest at first blush (sign of color) and bring them in to ripen at room temperature on the counter. Tomatoes do not need light to ripen, though it won't hurt to keep them out. While ripening, watch for fruit flies or any imperfections that could lead to spoilage. Once the tomatoes are ripe, process, eat, or freeze them, as most heirloom varieties won't keep long.

"Vine-ripened tomatoes" is a marketing term—in a grocery store, you're likely to find tomatoes that weren't actually vine ripened. This means they were harvested and shipped green and then treated with ethylene gas to cause them to turn red in transit or storage. Most tomatoes labeled as "vine-ripened" were likely picked on the vine and weren't fully ripe before shipping. That, plus cold storage, takes away from the flavor of grocery-store tomatoes, eliminating their natural taste and texture. Never keep your tomatoes in the refrigerator before processing them. If you're making sauce or salsa, you can keep them in the refrigerator, but when eating them fresh, refrigeration leads to a bland taste and grainy texture. If you slice a tomato and don't eat all of it, freeze the part you don't eat immediately to use for sauce or salsa. Putting half a tomato in the fridge will only lead to sadness and disappointment.

Picking tomatoes early can prevent bird damage like this.

CHERRY TOMATOES

Cherry tomatoes are ridiculously productive, but that doesn't mean you won't need a lot of them to make sauce. We don't recommend using only cherry tomatoes for sauce, because the skins cause bitterness. Cherry tomato plants are very productive, which is great when you have a lot of pest pressure, and they're great for snacking.

Cherry Tomato Varieties We Love

HYBRID

- Orange: 'Sunsugar'
- 'Super Sweet 100'
- Grape: 'Juliet'

HEIRLOOM

- Yellow: 'Galina', 'Yellow Pear'
- Red: 'Chadwick', 'Spoon', 'Small Red Cherry', 'Large Red Cherry'
- Pink: 'Pink Bumble Bee'
- Dark/purple: 'Blueberries', 'Indigo Cherry Drops', 'Chocolate Cherry Drops', 'Black Cherry'

There are a *lot* of cherry tomato varieties we haven't grown, because we don't need to grow as many cherry tomato plants. Twelve plants will yield a large mixing bowl full of cherry tomatoes almost daily through much of the season; some years we can get even more.

Preservation

Ways to preserve cherry tomatoes:

- Roasted cherry tomato salsa, canned tomato jam, freeze-dried (sliced in half) cherry tomatoes, frozen cherry tomatoes, and sun-dried (dehydrated) tomatoes.

Freeze-dried cherry tomatoes are a welcome taste of summer during the winter months.

- We freeze cherry tomatoes in vacuum-sealed freezer bags, in portions appropriate for thawing and baking in the oven with a bit of olive oil and Italian seasoning. After roasting, toss the cherry tomatoes in your favorite pasta with a bit of your favorite cheese for an easy pasta dish.
- Freeze-dried cherry tomatoes are great on salads and sandwiches, or they can be crushed into a powder and reconstituted into tomato paste.
- Roasted cherry tomato salsa is our favorite method for canning cherry tomatoes, but we often also throw some into our regular tomato sauce.

Water-bath canned tomato sauce

SAUCE TOMATOES

Sauce tomatoes have lower water content and generally have fewer seeds than other varieties. Most sauce tomatoes also have thicker skins, making them store a bit longer than heirloom slicers.

Sauce Tomato Varieties We Love

Our absolute favorite sauce tomato is made from the 'San Marzano' variety. They look like a Roma but have a much deeper, sweeter flavor. 'San Marzano' tomatoes make beautiful, bright red sauce. They're great sliced as a pizza topping or on sandwiches if you don't like a ton of tomato juice and seeds. Other favorite varieties are 'Amish Paste' and 'Jersey Devil'. While not as productive for us as the 'San Marzano', they're larger sauce tomatoes, making them worth growing if you like mixing things up.

Romas are our least favorite because they're determinates, growing all their tomatoes at once and then stopping for the season. This can be good for canning at one time, for short-season growing, or if you want more than one succession. Roma plants are also smaller than most other sauce tomatoes, so they may be a better choice for smaller spaces. They also don't need as much support or pruning.

As you may have guessed, the best way to preserve sauce tomatoes is by making sauce. Tomato paste is also an option, or homemade ketchup. They also make great salsa.

Tomatoes are acidic, so all canning options can be water-bath canned.

SLICER TOMATOES

We could write a whole book about the ins and outs of the tomato varieties we've grown, and slicers fall into the largest category. We grow a lot of slicers, on average fifteen to twenty varieties per year, at least two plants of each. Most years we add up to five new varieties to the list.

We'll break down our list of slicers by color. And note that a tomato's color isn't just a visual sign, it also represents flavor and texture.

Slicer Tomato Varieties We Love

- Black: 'Black Beauty', 'Blue Beauty'
- Black/purple: 'Cherokee Purple', 'Black from Tula', 'Black Krim'
- Green: We don't like green tomatoes. There, we said it.
- White: Really, a mild yellow: we've grown 'Giant White', but we don't include white tomatoes in our garden every year. These "white" tomatoes are more of a novelty item, as they don't have much flavor.
- Yellow: 'Dr. Whyche', 'Gold Medal', 'Pineapple', 'Kellogg's Breakfast'. 'Dr. Whyche' and 'Kellogg's Breakfast' are solid yellow tomatoes, large and meaty. 'Pineapple' and 'Gold Medal' are both large and yellow with red marbling. Sometimes 'Pineapple' turns almost entirely red, but there's still yellow somewhere inside.

Growing large slicers is almost as fun as eating them.

- Pink: Many pink tomatoes are noted for their meaty content, minimal seeds, and locule (the interior goo) content. This makes them ideal for holding their form on a sandwich. Some of our favorites include the 'Pink Brandywine' and 'Arkansas Traveler'.

We choose meaty slicer varieties, not only because we don't really like tomato seeds and the gooey locule, but because they can be more versatile: Slicers make great diced tomatoes, amazing sauce, tomato soup, and salsa.

Preservation

Slicers aren't just for slicing and eating fresh: they also make great sauce and salsa. Any tomato products can be freeze-dried, frozen, or dehydrated. Freeze-dried tomato slices are a fun addition to winter sandwiches: they're dry and crunchy, but you get the flavor of a fresh tomato—and it won't slip off your sandwich.

Dehydrated or freeze-dried tomato powder can be the base for a ready-to-make tomato paste for thickening sauces and soups. It's also tasty sprinkled on a creamy pasta.

Tomatoes can also be dehydrated to make sun-dried tomatoes.

BECOMING A BIG TOMATO EATER

If you're not a "big tomato eater," we want to encourage you to *try*. Most people who say they don't like fresh tomatoes are probably thinking of the subpar ones they've gotten at the grocery store or in restaurants. Sadly, many people only know tomatoes as pale, pink disks slapped on a fast-food hamburger.

Staci wasn't a big tomato eater, just a fan of cooked tomatoes and tomato soup and sauce. *Now* she's the biggest tomato snob. Not that she looks down her nose at any other type of produce, but it's possible to say she now lives for tomatoes. She has a personal rule not to eat store-bought tomato products of any kind.

If you want to become more of a tomato eater, try an heirloom slicer on a grilled cheese sandwich (bonus points if you milk the goat or cow and make the cheese yourself). Add a bit of basil salt or dill pickle salt (see recipe in the herb profile on page 113). There are few things we crave more, or that bring us more joy, than the first grilled-cheese-and-tomato sandwich after a long winter.

OKRA

Okra doesn't need a ton of space, and it doesn't need a trellis or support. Okra plants have tiny spines that can make people itch, so leave adequate space around them to minimize potential skin contact when you aren't harvesting. We plant our okra about 12 inches (30 cm) apart in a zigzag pattern. We plant a *lot* of okra (around forty plants per year) and we harvest a lot of okra, so this spacing works for us. Okra doesn't have any strong conventions for planting, so you can decide how you want to approach adding it to your garden.

The plant doesn't need to be pruned, just make sure to keep harvesting and it will keep producing.

PLANNING CONSIDERATIONS: Okra is native to east Africa, so it loves heat. In a hot climate it can be a prolific producer of its edible pods. Depending on the variety, the flowers are beautiful and will attract pollinators. We've tried starting okra in the greenhouse, which has resulted in sickly plants and no real advantage over direct sowing.

SUN REQUIREMENTS: Having originated in equatorial Africa, okra likes heat and sun.

PESTS: Besides some slug damage when they're young, okra plants don't suffer greatly from pest issues. Ants may eat the flower buds before they bloom, and if they get voracious the okra fruit that does develop will be deformed and curved. Aphids are also a nuisance: the insects like young okra pods as they are developing and will damage them when small, causing them to grow into odd shapes.

HARVESTING: Pick your okra daily if possible—the pods grow fast. Most okra should be harvested when the pod is just a little longer than your thumb. If you find your okra is tough, has large seeds, or makes a crunching sound when you cut it, that means you need to harvest it when it's smaller. Consider wearing gloves and long sleeves while harvesting okra, as the tiny hairs on okra plants can cause intense itching. You'll also likely get some slimy stuff on your fingers from the stems; while it can be messy, this slime (known as mucilage) is great for your gut and overall health.

VARIETIES WE LOVE

We've found that the 'Filipino Lady Fingers' variety fares better with ants and aphids than the more popular variety, 'Clemson Spineless' (which is not spineless, by the way, the spines are just harder to see). Unlike other plants we grow, we only have one variety of okra, 'Filipino Lady Fingers', which is our favorite. Finding okra seeds can be hard, so by only growing the one variety, we can easily save the seeds, which minimizes the chance of cross-pollination and preserves the variety standard. Red and orange okras (like 'Jing Orange' or 'Burgundy') can be fun to grow as well.

If you run out of ways to use okra for food, let the pods mature and use them for fall decor. If you miss a day picking okra, chickens also love overly mature okra (sometimes you need to slice it open for them).

PRESERVATION

Used fresh, we love okra in a stir-fry with other veggies like green beans, zucchini, and onions.

Okra is also great as an ingredient in soups, as its mucilage is a natural thickening agent that has been used for centuries in soups and gumbos.

↑ Freeze-dried okra slices

← ← Okra plants can get big, but they don't need much support.

← An okra harvest ready for preserving

OKRA FRIES

Wash your okra and remove the tops. Cut in quarters lengthwise and lay out on a baking sheet. Drizzle lightly with olive oil and sprinkle with herb salt. Bake at 350°F (180°C) for about 30 minutes or until brown, then enjoy as a crispy snack or as a dipper for hummus or your favorite dips.

We primarily freeze-dry okra in slices or sometimes quartered (with the stems removed). It holds its shape well when reconstituted and can even be breaded and fried after reconstituting.

If you don't have a freeze-dryer, you can slice or quarter okra pods and use vacuum seal bags to freeze it with good results. Dehydrated okra can be used in soups or stews as a thickener the same way you would use freeze-dried or frozen okra. As with many freeze-dried vegetables, add a bit of salt and turn your dehydrated or freeze-dried okra into a crunchy snack.

PEPPERS

Peppers can be pricey at the grocery store, and since they can be grown in small spaces, they're perfect for growing and preserving at home. Peppers do well in raised beds and containers, also in the ground. Our peppers tend to grow bigger and produce more when grown in raised beds, which also protect the plants from extremely wet conditions. We plant our peppers 6 to 8 inches (15 to 20 cm) apart in our raised beds, in a spot where they get shade in the late afternoon.

PLANNING CONSIDERATIONS: Peppers have good years and bad years, so don't get discouraged. Keep planting them every year. Try new varieties to find which ones do best for you, but don't judge them by a single growing season unless they obviously don't do well, or you don't like their flavor. Because of the tendency to have good and bad pepper years, when we have a good pepper year we preserve a *lot* of peppers. This creates the buffer we discussed in the planning section of the book (see sidebar, page 15). For example, 2023 was an amazing pepper year for our garden: we

↑ Preparing for pepper preservation.

← Shishito peppers are some of our favorites.

grew hundreds of plants and they all produced crazy amounts of peppers. In contrast, 2024 was not a great pepper year. Wet conditions followed by extremely dry conditions led to relatively few peppers.

The quantities you grow will depend on how you want to use them. You never know if you'll have enough jalapeños to can from one plant or if you'll need ten plants. If you didn't grow enough jalapeños to make pickled jalapeños, consider making hot sauce or jalapeño jelly, which won't take as many peppers. As a general rule, we plant ten to fifteen jalapeños, five to ten other, spicier peppers for hot sauces and pickled spicy peppers, and around sixty sweet pepper plants.

While pepper plants are drought tolerant, they have their limits—especially in raised beds and containers. To keep them producing, make sure they get regular watering. Peppers can take a long time to ripen, so be patient! We plant our peppers from seed in the greenhouse in March, then plant them out when overnight temperatures are above 55°F (13°C); for us, that's in the second half May. We typically don't harvest ripe peppers until early August, though green peppers will be ready before that. Some varieties are traditionally picked green, including jalapeños, green bell peppers, banana peppers, and shishitos. Other varieties ripen to an array of colors.

SUN REQUIREMENTS: Peppers need at least eight hours of sun per day. If you live in a hot climate (with temperatures over 85°F [29°C] most of the summer), consider planting your peppers where they get some afternoon shade while still receiving morning sun.

GROWING SEASON: Summer. Peppers are frost tender. We always put our peppers in the ground as soon as we feel the threat of frost has passed, which is early May for us.

PESTS: Peppers are nightshades, so their pests are similar to those that attack other nightshade crops, such tomatoes, potatoes, and eggplants. If the soil is too cool or too rich in nitrogen when they're planted, aphids can become a problem. While tomato hornworms prefer tomatoes, they will also attack peppers: if you see defoliation, you may have hornworms. Whenever you suspect that you have these pests, remember that they will glow if you shine a black light on them, which makes them easy to spot in the dark.

HARVESTING: We don't prune our pepper plants, though many people believe you should "top" them. This method, also called pinching, removes the top of the young plant when it has six to eight sets of true leaves. Doing this forces the plant to branch out sooner, causing the plant to produce more branches and therefore more fruits. In a situation where you have a long growing season, this may work for some people, but for us it just delays production. Your results will vary based on your climate.

VARIETIES WE LOVE

Sweet peppers

These are our top four highest producing heirloom sweet pepper varieties. These pepper types produce the most for us, whereas our bell peppers tend to be less prolific.

- **'BLOT'**: An oblong bell pepper that ripens to a beautiful sunset color
- **'LESYA'**: Heart-shaped, thick-walled, extremely sweet
- **'JIMMY NARDELLO'**: A long, slender sweet pepper, great for adding to soups, stir-fries, and casseroles
- **BANANA PEPPERS**: Mild yet distinctive flavor, not as sweet as the others

Note that there are also spicy banana peppers, so don't mix them up, unless you're looking for a spicy pepper. Banana peppers ripen to red, even though many people pick them when they are a light lime-green color. If you plan on pickling them, they'll have more crunch when they're lime green when you harvest them.

Spicy Peppers

- **JALAPEÑOS**: A traditionally prolific hot pepper that matures to a deep green, purple, or red, depending on the subtype
- **THAI CHILIS**: Small but powerful, a single plant can grow hundreds of tiny peppers that pack a punch
- **GHOST PEPPER**: Incredibly spicy bonnet pepper that tends to grow prolifically

↑ Spicy pickled jalapeño peppers

← Our kids love to grow different kinds of peppers. They're bright, colorful, and fun to experiment with.

Mildly Spicy Peppers

- **PEPPERONCINI**: Great for pickling and using in roasts and chili
- **'ANAHEIM'**: A good munching pepper, growing several inches long with a firm flesh
- **SHISHITO**: An east Asian pepper, a heavy producer

A note on shishitos: most are extremely mild, but every once in a while you'll find one with a little heat. They're small, have a petite, thin flesh, and are great in stir-fry dishes.

PRESERVATION

Thai chili peppers and other small chili peppers dry well. You can use a needle and thread to string them up by their stems and hang them to dry, and they also do well drying when laid out on a baking sheet. If you live in a dry climate, you may be able to hang dried cayenne or chili peppers as well. Larger, fleshier peppers will not air-dry well when the climate is consistently humid.

Nearly all peppers are great for freeze-drying, freezing, or dehydrating; you can make them into paprika, chili flakes, or other variations. We use the sweet bell-type peppers to make our own paprika by dehydrating them and grinding them into powder in a food processor. Shishitos are one of our favorite peppers to freeze-dry, which we add to stir-fry dishes year-round. Freeze-dried peppers can be used in recipes just as you would frozen peppers, or they can be used as a veggie chip for dipping.

Pickled peppers are also popular in our house. Pickled jalapeños, pickled banana peppers, pickled pepperoncini, and pickled Thai chilis always have a spot in our pantry. They're great on nachos, make a winning addition to a bowl of chili, or offer zest to an otherwise boring soup. Above all, we love sweet pickled jalapeños, otherwise known as Cowboy Candy. You can also create hot sauce from them, basically blending sweet pickled peppers.

While pickled peppers offer an easy starting place when preserving peppers, our absolute favorite for spicy peppers is the sweet and spicy hot sauce recipe above.

SWEET AND SPICY HOT SAUCE

You can leave the seeds in *or* take them out, according to your taste.

INGREDIENTS

½ pound (227 g) chopped peppers (hot or spicy, depending on your taste)

2 cups (474 ml) vinegar

2 cups (400 g) sugar

2 cups (474 ml) water

1 or more clove garlic

INSTRUCTIONS

Simmer 30 to 60 minutes on medium to low heat until peppers are soft.

Blend with your immersion blender.

Cook down on low heat until half the original volume.

You can add ClearJel as an option to thicken your sauce at the end (make a slurry with water and then add it or it will clump up), but we usually skip this step as it is thick enough for us after cooking down.

We normally water-bath can this recipe for 20 minutes for half-pints (237 ml) or 30 minutes for pints (473 ml). Note that this is not a tested recipe, but with the vinegar and sugar we treat it like a pepper jelly or pepper relish.

GREEN BEANS

This profile applies to beans that are eaten within the pods. We call them green beans, but the colloquial name for them varies regionally (snap beans, string beans, etc.). Don't confuse them with dry beans, which are the individual beans that grow inside of the pods and are consumed as such (we'll cover dry beans in the next profile). When growing green beans, focus on your preservation goals, space, pest pressure, and other factors.

There are bush-types and climbing pole-types of green beans. Bush beans can be planted closely together in spaced rows, but these can take up a lot of space depending on how many you plan to grow. Pole beans can be grown vertically, which saves space, especially in smaller gardens. They produce a similar final product, but consider that pole beans take up to seventy days to mature, while bush beans take forty to sixty days.

↑ "Green" beans come in a variety of different colors, but all will turn green after being canned.

← Young bush bean plants thriving in a raised bed

↙ Green beans are easy to grow and to pick.

PLANNING CONSIDERATIONS: We succession plant our bush beans because we require such a large yield to meet our preservation goals (see chapter 3). If you have hot summers, green beans will do much better in the spring and fall. When temperatures are over 85°F (29°C), pollination is reduced. Beans are self pollinating, but that means they don't tolerate heat well (something to consider if you want to use nets to deter pests). That said, some varieties are more heat tolerant than others—in general, when researching varieties, if the writeup doesn't mention heat tolerance, the variety probably isn't. We've had good luck with 'Provider' and 'Goldilocks' bush beans for high-producing, heat-tolerant varieties, though temperatures over 95°F (35°C) in the high summer will still knock down production on any varieties we've seen. When beans do bloom in extremely high heat, the pods may be underdeveloped, curved, or extremely small.

SUN REQUIREMENTS: Full sun. At least six to eight hours per day is required.

GROWING SEASON: Summer.

PESTS: We rarely have issues with pests attacking our green beans, but we know that is not the norm in all areas.

Our top four pests for green beans are aphids, cutworms, slugs, and (for pole beans) Japanese beetles. Once the plants have a couple sets of true leaves, we usually don't have any further issues with pest damage. If you live in an area where bean beetles are an issue, we encourage you to do further research on controlling them. Though Japanese beetles can be a major pest for pole beans, they seem to leave bush beans alone. As with other crops that Japanese beetles like to munch on, your best bet is to knock them off into a jar of soapy water. Know that, if your plants are healthy and thriving before the beetles arrive in the summer, the insects will just munch the leaves on top but won't affect the harvest significantly.

HARVESTING: If you're looking to preserve your beans in smaller batches—such as freezing either for later freeze-drying or to eat out of the freezer over the winter—planting pole beans may work for you. A 20-foot (6 m) long row of pole beans will produce enough beans to blanch and freeze each week, but it may not produce a whole canner-load a week (it depends on what varieties you plant). Bush beans, on the other hand, produce a *lot* of beans all at once, so a similar planting could produce enough beans to fill your canner multiple times per week, but over a shorter time period.

Harvesting pole beans is physically easier, especially if you don't like to bend and squat: when they grow up a trellis or fence, you can stand up while picking. Bush beans grow along the ground, reaching only about 18 inches (46 cm) tall. Some people pick all their bush beans only once or twice per planting, and some even pull the plants and take the beans off, getting only one harvest from their bush beans (but saving the back pain). Unless they're going to die anyway (from frost or some other condition), we prefer to get the most out of our plants by harvesting our bush beans three or four times a week while they're producing.

Pole beans tend to be more tolerant of heat and produce over a longer period of time. They take up more vertical space, can be planted close together in the ground, and do well in containers and raised beds or in the ground. It's a good idea to succession plant pole beans if you want to keep harvesting throughout the season.

Whichever bean you have, keep harvesting so that your plants will produce more. Like any plant, once the seed is produced the plant slows down bloom production to focus on maturing the seeds.

VARIETIES WE LOVE

Pole Beans

- 'Old Homestead' (a.k.a. 'Kentucky Wonder Pole')
- 'McCaslan 42'
- 'Purple Podded'

Bush Beans

- 'Dragon Tongue'
- 'Bamako'
- 'Provider'

PRESERVING

The four most reliable ways to preserve green beans are freezing, pressure canning, freeze-drying, and pickling. Freshly picked green beans will keep for a week or two in a plastic bag or sealed container in the refrigerator, so you can build up enough to can or freeze-dry a full batch.

When freezing, the beans need to be snapped and blanched, then frozen in vacuum-sealed bags. To blanch, dunk the beans into boiling water for one to two minutes (the time required depends on the size of the beans), then dry them and freeze. You can freeze your beans on a baking sheet and then put the frozen pods into freezer bags or, for better results, use vacuum bags. You can pre-freeze them on the baking sheet or just put them straight into the vacuum bag—though results will be better if they're already frozen, which avoids squishing them in the vacuum bag. Frozen beans can be thawed and used as if fresh.

We prefer to freeze-dry our green beans. You get a similar flavor, texture, and use as you do with frozen beans, but they're shelf stable and won't take up space in your freezer. Another bonus for freeze-drying beans: you don't need to blanch them. To freeze-dry your beans, snap off the ends and freeze-dry. We generally store freeze-dried green beans in glass canning jars, then reconstitute them with hot tap water (not boiling) for stir-frying or casseroles. Like so many freeze-dried vegetables, beans taste great as a crunchy snack.

Pressure canning beans is required for traditional canning, rather than using a water-bath, because of the low acid content of green beans.

You can also pickle green beans, using them in place of cucumbers or other vegetables in vinegar. Dilly beans are popular with our kids!

For dehydrated green beans, you can dry your beans any way you like. One caveat: if you use an air-drying method without a dehydrator, watch out for mold.

It was common for many years in the South to string up green beans on a thread. These dehydrated beans were called leather britches, and when you see a batch you'll know why.

Maybe you remember eating mushy green beans that were cooked all day long with a bit of bacon or ham for flavor. While in more recent years people throw their canned or frozen beans in the pot and completely overcook them, simmering the beans for hours until they're completely tender, dehydrated beans have to be cooked on the stove in a bit of broth or water in order to return them to an edible state. Whether beans need to be overcooked or not is up to you. Personally, we prefer the taste of fresh, lightly cooked or steamed green beans that still hold their fresh flavor. Cooking them all day with a bit of bacon, ham, or bacon grease does result in a dish people like, and it's a comfort food that many actually love. We encourage you to save your beans for winter or for using a new-to-you storage method of dehydrating your green beans.

Pressure canned and freeze-dried green beans, side by side

DRY BEANS

Growing conditions and requirements are the same for both green and dry beans, but there's a difference: when you stop harvesting your green beans, they'll eventually mature and produce dry seed, but you'll get better food production if you grow varieties specially bred to produce dry beans. With all the effort it takes to hull beans by hand, growing dry bean varieties will result in beans with a more normal size and shape per pod than simply letting green beans mature.

If you want to save seeds (rather than saving beans to eat), it makes more sense to let your other varieties mature. When planting for the purpose of growing dry beans to eat, it's better to use a variety that was bred for dry beans, as they will often have a thicker, tougher pod, or more strings than varieties that were bred to make a tender green bean. Plant dry beans in places where they can be left alone to mature and dry, whether pole or bush.

PLANNING CONSIDERATIONS: Don't plant dry beans *with* your green beans. Though this might be confusing, trust us: we've made this mistake. There are dual-purpose varieties available, but they tend to produce low-quality dry beans, or tougher, stringier green beans. So we prefer to keep ours separate to get the best of both types of beans.

← Dry bean plants in the garden

Nevertheless, we have a couple of favorite varieties that offer a good dual-purpose option if you want to grow both, especially if your growing space is limited.

Like green beans, there are both bush and pole types of dry beans. Most dry bean bush varieties have plants that produce their beans all at once, much like green bush varieties. The whole plant will typically be covered in beans that start out green, then yellow as the beans inside dry. Bush beans can be planted close together, 4 to 6 inches (10 to 15 cm) apart works well. In the past, we consistently got 1 quart (946 ml) jar full of dry beans from fifty seeds (dry bush bean plants). This amount, however, will vary a bit based on variety, weather, soil conditions, and other factors.

Last year, we planted our bush-type dry beans in a raised bed. We were able to fit over two hundred dry bush bean plants in a 6-by-3-foot (1.8-by-0.9-m) raised bed, in a smaller, more out-of-the-way space. Some of them did vine, as often happens with heirloom dry bush beans. These were all heirloom varieties with an assortment of fun colors.

SUN REQUIREMENTS: Full sun.

GROWING SEASON: Summer.

PESTS: See the description of pests in the green bean profile section on page 101.

HARVEST: Let the pods and beans dry on the plant. Once the bean pods start to dry out and feel leathery, pull the entire plant out and hang it in a covered area to dry. This protects your beans from pests and the rain. There have been some years when my dry beans were almost mature and then we had a soaking rain, which led to one of two problems: either the pods become mildewed (usually harmless) or sometimes the beans actually developed mold. The worse scenario was when, if the moisture and temperatures were just right (or wrong), the dry beans would sprout in their pods!

BEANS BEFORE FROST

If frost is in the forecast and you're growing dry beans pick all the pods and use these not-yet-mature and not-yet-dry beans to make soup. In our house, we make chili around the time of our first frost using the last of the tomatoes, peppers, and fresh beans (we add the last pods left on the plant that won't have time to dry or mature before they freeze). These almost-mature beans taste amazing once cooked in your chili; since they aren't completely dry, you don't have to soak or precook them. We simmer them on the stovetop for several hours while cooking down (reducing) the tomato sauce in the chili. Make sure your beans aren't already starting to dry or you'll need to add a step for traditional soaking and precooking. The beans need to be in their still-green pods.

VARIETIES WE LOVE

Dual-Purpose Beans

We know we said to keep dry beans and green beans separate, but our favorite dual-purpose beans are the 'Cherokee Trail of Tears' pole bean and '1500 Year Old Cave'.

Dry Beans

- Navy (bush)
- Pinto (bush or pole, check your seeds)
- 'Black Turtle' (bush)
- 'Mbombo' (bush)
- 'Turkey Craw' (pole)

PRESERVATION

To preserve dry beans, all you have to do is let them dry, which makes the process easy. After they're dry, get them out of their shells—this can take a fair amount of time, but at least it can be done later (in our case, sometimes years later). While leaving them in this form isn't great for space efficiency, dry beans do keep indefinitely indoors in their pods or shells.

WINTER SQUASH

Winter squash is one of the largest plants you can grow in your garden. They need space to spread on the ground, or they can be grown vertically on a trellis.

PLANNING CONSIDERATIONS: Different varieties produce a different average number of fruits. Many pumpkin varieties only produce one or two fruits per plant each season. The varieties we recommend tend to produce much more: ten to fifteen fruits per plant is not uncommon. It can be difficult to plan for the yield, because some years this number may be much less. Because of the long shelf life and easy, versatile preservation methods you have with winter squash, I recommend planting as many as you have room for each year. That way, if you have a good year, you can store extra squash and not go without during a bad year.

SUN REQUIREMENT: Full sun.

GROWING SEASON: Summer. Frost tender. Winter squash typically need between 100 and 120 days to mature.

PESTS: Squash bugs, vine borers, cucumber beetles

HARVEST: Ideally, you should wait to harvest until either the stem has started to dry or it passes the fingernail test. To conduct a fingernail test, puncture, or attempt to puncture, the skin on the stem end of the squash. If it's hard and you can't easily puncture it with your fingernail, the squash is ready for harvest.

Leave the stem attached when harvesting a winter squash. If you're dealing with pests, extreme heat, or a pending frost, harvest winter squash when they're still green and not quite ready. If fully grown, they will still ripen indoors, but their shelf life may be impacted. By waiting until the squash is fully ripened, you can extend its shelf life. If you just want to save your squash from an impending frost or pest pressure, harvest it a bit early. If you can wait until the squash has fully matured on the vine, however, many varieties have a shelf life of over six months at room temperature.

VARIETIES WE LOVE

- **'LONG ISLAND CHEESE' PUMPKIN:** This is a solid-stem pumpkin, which means it's resistant to vine borers and lasts in our food storage pantry for at least nine months.
- **ZUCCHINO RAMPICANTE (A.K.A. TROMBONCINO):** Another solid-stem favorite with an amazing shelf life. This variety pulls double-duty in the garden! When young and tender, about a foot long, it can be eaten like a zucchini. If you continue to harvest the young fruits, the vines will continue producing. If you stop harvesting, the plants set a few very large squash that resemble a butternut, with a long curved neck and thicker skin.
- **'SEMINOLE' PUMPKIN:** A great choice for gardeners who live in hot, humid climates. This variety is resistant to squash vine borers, squash bugs, and produces heavily. It thrives late in summer when other varieties can slow down due to the heat.

↑ Regardless of the variety, most winter squash can be processed similarly for immediate use or long-term storage.

← Winter squash straight from the garden

PRESERVATION

With a long shelf life at room temperature, winter squash may not need to be formally preserved. When you notice the fruit starting to wrinkle a little, or if you know you have more than you'll be able to eat in six months, it's time to decide what to do.

Any preservation method for winter squash begins with cooking. The squash can be cut in half or into otherwise manageable pieces after removing the seeds and guts, then bake or steam the flesh. You can use an oven, a slow cooker, or a pressure cooker to cook it. Remove the skin prior to cooking or leave the skin on and remove it after the cooked squash has cooled.

Our favorite preservation method for winter squash is freeze-drying. Freezing or dehydrating are methods that also work well. We purée the cooked flesh and either put it in the freeze-dryer, freeze it in freezer bags or vacuum bags, or dehydrate it. With the freeze-dryer, the resulting product is soft enough to crush with a spoon into a powder. Likewise, after drying with a dehydrator, you can derive a powder from the dried flesh using your blender. The powder can be stored in Mylar bags or in canning jars that have been sealed tightly. An oxygen absorber will help increase shelf life. The squash powder can be reconstituted with water and used to make pumpkin bread or to thicken soups. Cooked winter squash can also be cubed and freeze-dried or frozen for use in stews, casseroles, or other recipes.

← Zucchino rampicante fruits are some of our favorites because of their versatility.

PUMPKIN BREAD

Pumpkin bread is a year-round staple in our house. It is a great bread for breakfast, and a quick treat anytime it's on the counter.

INGREDIENTS

Dry

1⅔ cups (208 g) flour (can use a gluten-free flour mix)

1 teaspoon baking soda

½ teaspoon baking powder

¾ teaspoon salt

1½ teaspoons pumpkin pie spice

Wet

1 cup (245 g) pumpkin or squash puree (fresh or reconstituted)

½ cup (119 ml) water or milk

½ cup (119 ml) neutral oil

2 eggs

1⅓ cups (267 g) sugar

¾ cup (131 g) chocolate chips (optional)

INSTRUCTIONS

Preheat the oven to 350°F (180°C) and prepare a 9 x 5-inch (23 x 13 cm) bread pan.

Whisk together all the dry ingredients in a large bowl.

Mix together all the wet ingredients in a medium bowl.

Add the wet ingredients to the dry ones and mix until just combined.

Fold in the chocolate chips and transfer to the prepared bread pan

Bake for 45 to 60 minutes or until a toothpick comes out clean. Allow to cool completely before slicing.

HERBS

Herbs cover a wide range of plants and preparations. We can generalize a bit and say that most herbs grow well in containers and small spaces, and even indoors with adequate light. They are also simple to preserve by dehydrating, freezing, or freeze-drying. Herbs can also be included in your other preservation and canning recipes.

Many people don't think about preserving herbs as part of their food preservation strategy, but nothing tastes as good without them. (Plus, anything you can grow will taste better than buying it at the store.)

Of all the herb preservation methods, freeze-drying is my favorite. I do use air-drying and make herb salts frequently as well, but freeze-dried herbs taste like fresh herbs and are easy to crumble over your food. Freeze-dried herbs maintain more of their essential oils, which give them the strongest flavor, and they stay truer to their original color, retaining their brightness and vibrancy. If you don't freeze-dry your herbs, air-drying is your next best alternative. You can use a dehydrator, but be sure to use ambient temperatures, as any high temperatures will just cook the herbs and result in a disappointing brown powder.

Freeze-dried dill

BASIL

How much basil is enough? It depends not only on your family size and preferences but on your climate. If you only grow *one* herb, grow basil: it's versatile and doesn't require pampering. If you're preserving by air-drying or freezing, you can harvest and preserve basil continuously throughout the season. To grow large amounts of basil (which we want), we plant thirty to forty plants each year, which allows us wiggle room if we miss a harvest: enough basil to eat fresh all summer, some for pesto we can freeze, some for a large batch of basil salt, and then more that we preserve as 4 to 6 quarts (1.2 to 1.7 kg) of crushed, freeze-dried basil. Adjust the number of plants to suit your own climate and growing conditions. Once you've had homegrown basil, you won't settle for anything else!

PLANNING CONSIDERATIONS: Basil is an annual that prefers to be grown in full sun. Think tropical conditions: 80°F (27°C) with lows above 60°F (16°C). Though it won't completely die until it freezes, basil doesn't enjoy cool nights and will not thrive if the sustained temperature is too low.

Plan to plant basil at about the same time you would plant tomatoes and other summer crops. Here in southern Missouri, we plant basil outside around Mother's Day, about two weeks after our last frost date. While it will live outside when the nights are cool, basil won't tolerate a freeze or frost, nor will it thrive until overnight temperatures are above 60°F (16°C). Basil can also be grown in patio containers, indoors in a sunny, south-facing window, or under grow lights.

Basil needs warm soil to germinate, so use a heat mat or other heat source to warm up the soil to 70°F to 80°F (21°C to 27°C). If you're starting basil indoors, and your house is around 70°F (21°F), remember that your soil temperature without a heat mat can run 10°F to 15°F (6°C to 8°C) cooler than the room temperature.

Basil is easily grown from cuttings: Remove the lower leaves and place the cuttings in water, then wait for roots to sprout.

SUN REQUIREMENTS: Full sun.

GROWING SEASON: Summer. Basil is not frost tolerant.

HARVESTING: Basil should be harvested before the plants go to flower by removing either individual leaves or entire stems (see sidebar). Make your cuts just above a set of leaves and the plant will branch and generate future harvests.

VARIETIES WE LOVE

Among the many different basil varieties, our favorites include lemon basil, cinnamon basil, Thai basil, and 'Genovese' basil. Each has its own flavor and is well suited to its own use. We like to use Thai basil when cooking Asian foods, lemon basil for Mexican dishes and chicken, and 'Genovese' basil as a great all-around basil that's good in pesto and just about everything.

PRUNING BASIL

Pinching the tips of your basil will help it grow bushier, producing more leaves. Some people believe that the flavor of basil changes once it flowers—*we are not those people*. While tender young plants are nearly always at least a little bit better, there's no reason not to eat or preserve your basil after it has "bolted" (bloomed). We simply pinch off the flowers and only preserve the leaves.

Beyond freeze-drying, we use most of our basil for basil salt.

PRESERVING

Basil is the utility player herb in our kitchen, largely because of its versatility. A tasty addition in pretty much any savory dish—fresh, dried, or dried in salt to make a flavored herb salt—you can add basil or basil-infused salt to French fries, baked potatoes, scrambled eggs, soup, chili, pasta, or casseroles.

Freeze-drying basil gives you the best option for preservation. You get the flavor and color of fresh basil in an easy-to-use, shelf-stable package. You can even rehydrate freeze-dried basil and use it to make pesto.

Basil can also be frozen. It's best to vacuum seal it: if you don't, you should know that any part of the leaves exposed to cold and oxygen in the freezer will turn black. This doesn't change the flavor, but it's not very pretty.

Since canning pesto isn't a safe option at home, we freeze ours in ice-cube trays and transfer the frozen cubes to freezer bags for easy portioning. It's best to use these within six months or vacuum seal them.

Basil can also be dehydrated or hung to dry. Once dry on the stems, place the dry basil stems with leaves on a cookie sheet and crush them gently.

BASIL SALT

We use basil salts in a shaker on our counter instead of plain salt when cooking or as a table seasoning.

To make basil salt, pick the leaves off your plant and remove as many of the larger stems as possible. Wash the leaves thoroughly and gently pat them dry, but don't worry about getting them completely dry: a little moisture will help in the next steps. When you have about 1 cup (24 g) of compressed leaves, put them in your food processor and blend them into a paste. If it's too thick and will not blend, add water a tiny bit at a time to aid in the blending process. Once it looks like a thick green paste, set your blender to a very low setting and add kosher salt in small amounts until you can see both green from the basil and white flakes from the salt.

Once there's enough salt mixed in for you to easily remove the mixture from the blender, dump it into a bowl. Add more salt and stir with a spoon: this keeps the salt from becoming too fine for the blender; if you prefer a fine salt, continue blending and skip this step. The more salt you add, the lighter the color and flavor will be. How much you should add depends on your personal taste. When you finish, the product will be similar to wet sand (not a paste). At this point, place it in thin layers (½ inch [1 cm] or less) on a dehydrator tray and dehydrate on the lowest setting possible until no moisture remains. It's important to do this with as little heat as possible: heat will damage the basil and cause it to turn brown.

If you don't have a dehydrator, you can do this on sheet pans in your oven with the oven light on. This process takes a day or two, but will be effective as long as you don't turn the oven on. If you live in a dry climate, you can just leave the trays of basil out with a fan blowing on them, which will be enough to dry out your salt.

Once the basil salt is dry, store it in tightly closed canning jars and transfer a small amount to a shaker or other countertop container. When storing, keep the jars out of direct sunlight, as light will cause the basil to fade over time.

ROSEMARY

Rosemary is a great garden herb for preserving. Most people are underwhelmed by this herb because they've only had overdried, overprocessed rosemary bought in a grocery store. Fresh, properly preserved rosemary is lovely and super fragrant! It grows on a woody stem, and the individual leaves are tough and woody as well. They can be used as a flavorful aromatic seasoning, but generally rosemary is too tough to eat unprepared.

We grow this herb in our garden as an annual, but it can be planted in a container and brought inside for the winter, then put back outside in the spring. Some varieties are hardier in cold weather than others, but we've never found a variety that produces consistently and survives our winters. It's still worth growing your own rosemary, as it can grow well in one season. One plant typically produces a 1-quart (946 ml) jar or two of rosemary sprigs, loosely packed. We grow about five to ten rosemary plants each year. With this amount we can have enough to eat fresh all season and into the fall, and still dry two to four quart jars (946 ml) of rosemary sprigs.

We dedicated an entire raised bed to rosemary last year.

PLANNING CONSIDERATIONS: Rosemary prefers full sun and warm temperatures, but not extremely hot or wet weather. Rosemary can be prone to root rot. It's important to let the soil dry between waterings, and for this reason it's often grown in containers or raised beds. Germination can be difficult, so buying rosemary as a planted start is recommended. In fact, think of rosemary more like a succulent or cactus.

SUN REQUIREMENTS: As with other herbs, rosemary likes full sun and will do well in a pot on a south-facing windowsill. It will grow in proportion to the size of its pot.

GROWING SEASON: When planted in the spring, rosemary will grow slowly. You may think it's stalling out, but when the temperatures get warm enough, it will shoot up dramatically. If you live in a hot climate, plant your rosemary where it will get some afternoon shade.

HARVESTING: Cut branches from the plant when they are several inches long. The more frequently you harvest, the more branches your plant will produce. For immediate use, remove individual leaves or just pinch off the stem tips.

Dried rosemary stored in a glass screw-top jar

VARIETIES WE LOVE

While there are many varieties of rosemary, they can generally be classified as either upright, groundcover, or creeping. We've grown several varieties of upright and have been happy with most of them. We have yet to find a rosemary variety that will overwinter in our climate—if we did, it would be an automatic favorite.

PRESERVATION

The easiest way to preserve rosemary is to cut off 3- to 4-inch (7.5 to 10 cm) branches and lay them out on a flat surface. They'll air-dry indoors in just a week or two and can then be stored in an airtight container. You can also freeze-dry rosemary, which preserves more of its color and fresh flavor. Freeze-dried rosemary is still bright green and looks and tastes exactly as it did on the plant.

ENJOYING ROSEMARY

One of our favorite ways to eat rosemary is as an aromatic in beef and pork dishes. Its piney aroma balances the subtle flavors of pork, so we use a sprig of rosemary to season a pork tenderloin or a steak.

This method can be used in a slow cooker (but not in an Instant Pot, as high-temperature pressure cooking can often ruin the flavor of herbs). We've had the best results with a sous-vide cooker, an appliance that heats water around the food so that it slowly brings it to a specific temperature.

To cook this dish with a sous vide, we seal a tenderloin in a vacuum seal bag with a little bit of basil salt, garlic, and rosemary. Then we place it in our sous vide cooker to cook to about 150°F (66°C) for pork, then slice and sear the tenderloin after removing the rosemary. The intense flavor permeates the meat for a wonderful final taste. The same technique can be used for a beefsteak such as a ribeye, T-bone, sirloin, or any other cut; the main difference is that we cook beef to 137°F (58°C) in the sous vide, which is an ideal medium temperature.

We also include a sprig of rosemary in a pot roast. We cook a chuck roast in the slow cooker on low for 12 to 18 hours with rosemary, garlic, sliced onion, basil salt, and a pint of sugar-free applesauce. The result is a sweet and savory meat that falls apart on the fork.

Lastly, rosemary can be used in soups and stews. Remember that it's woody and will not go well in these dishes unless you grind it, otherwise you should remove the sticks before serving your finished dish.

DILL

A handful of fresh dill leaves

Dill is one of our favorite herbs to grow: we use it in many preservation recipes.

PLANNING CONSIDERATIONS: Dill can be planted close together, with just a ¼ inch (6 mm) spacing between seedlings. Start dill in early spring, as soon as the soil is workable, or start it indoors and transplant outside. Starting seedlings for transplant can lead to quicker germination. If you let dill go to seed in your garden, chances are good you'll have volunteer dill the following season. The seedlings can handle the frost, but the seeds won't always germinate as quickly if the temperatures are cold.

SUN REQUIREMENT: Full sun.

GROWING SEASON: Dill is a cold-hardy annual. It may grow in the fall and through the winter in warmer climates, but in our garden we plant it in the early spring. It is frost tolerant when young and tends to die back after blooming in the heat of summer. In a mild summer, it will grow again when the weather cools down, continuing into early fall.

HARVESTING: Snip off individual leaves for fresh use or preservation. Let some of the plant go to flower and save a ½ pint (106 g) or more of dried dill seed (also used for culinary purposes).

VARIETIES WE LOVE

There are several varieties of dill. We grow 'Bouquet' dill for the long-stem flowers and large seedheads, and 'Tetra' dill for its bushy growth habit and abundant leaves. Dill can be interplanted with squash and other vegetables to help prevent pests. Its blossoms attract pollinators and parasitic wasps that help to control hornworms and other caterpillars in the garden. We used to plant our dill between tomato plants, but have since learned from companion planting guidelines that this will stunt tomato growth as the dill matures. Personally, we've never experienced this, but if you're new to gardening, do as we say, not as we do.

We grow a lot of dill, mostly because we can. It's easy to grow, doesn't require a lot of hands-on care, deters pests, and doesn't take up much space. We also love it because pollinators love it, as dill is a host plant for black swallowtail butterflies. It's also a great filler for flower bouquets.

PRESERVATION

For preservation purposes, having over thirty dill plants will give you enough to preserve for herb salts, use in ranch seasoning or pickles, and have enough left over for 1 or 2 quarts (198 or 397 g) of dried dill. (Thirty plants may sound like a lot, but remember that they can be direct-seeded and planted as close as ¼ inch [6 mm] apart.) If you live in a hot climate, you may want to plant your dill early and experiment with yields; if your cool season is short, you may need to plant a lot more.

If not using the dill directly in other preservation methods, you can dry it (air-dried or dehydrated at 100°F [38°C] or lower) or freeze-dry it. As with other herbs, we prefer to freeze-dry dill.

Dill can also be preserved as an herb salt, as discussed above in the basil profile.

Pickling is the most popular use for dill, and this is also a standard method for preserving this herb. Dill pickles typically mean pickled cucumbers, but we've been known to pickle everything from green beans to garlic, from carrots to hard-boiled quail eggs.

DILL FOR POLLINATORS

A black swallowtail caterpillar on carrot greens

Remember that dill is one of the most desired host plants for black swallowtail butterflies while in their caterpillar state. They also love carrot greens, fennel, and parsley. These are beautiful tenants in your garden, even if only temporarily. We always plant extra dill plants to make sure we have enough to share with the butterflies. If you find their caterpillars munching on these plants, consider moving them all to a "sacrifice area" where you don't plan to harvest the host plant. Since we don't use our fennel except for the seeds, we move our swallowtail caterpillars to the fennel plants so they can happily eat and not disturb our other plants. If we run out of fennel, we sacrifice some carrot greens: as long as the carrots aren't brand-new, they can handle the damage and will regrow. An even better alternative is to find Queen Anne's lace or wild carrot on your property and move the caterpillars there (make sure to properly identify this plant and know that it is invasive in the United States—you shouldn't plant Queen Anne's lace intentionally.)

CILANTRO

Cilantro seeds = coriander

Cilantro is one of those tastes that you either love or hate—there isn't a lot of middle ground. Cilantro contains aldehyde, a naturally occurring compound found in the leaves. While most people don't perceive it, some can taste the soap-flavored aldehydes. Julia Child was a famously outspoken cilantro hater and never had a nice thing to say about it. Luckily for us, our family lacks the genetic variation that makes cilantro taste like soap, and we love it! We grow cilantro for fresh eating and preservation.

PLANNING CONSIDERATIONS: When considering how much cilantro to plant, consider two main things. One, that you'll likely want cilantro to use with tomato-based salsa dishes and, by the time tomatoes are ripe, cilantro will likely have bolted. Second, consider that if cilantro is allowed to go to seed, it will self-seed all over your garden. If you planted cilantro and it flowered, you may not need to plant any at all the following year. The tiny flowers on cilantro are also great for attracting beneficial insects.

SUN REQUIREMENTS: Full sun in spring, partial shade in summer.

GROWING SEASON: Cilantro enjoys cool but sunny weather. It will flower when temperatures increase, so get it started and planted out in the spring when the weather is still cool.

HARVESTING: Cilantro leaves can be cut from the plant in the spring at any time before it flowers. After flowering, its taste will become more bitter.

The seeds of the cilantro plant, coriander, are a bonus you get when you grow cilantro. They dry easily on the plant and can be easily collected—just don't collect them all or you won't have any volunteer cilantro plants next year.

VARIETIES WE LOVE

If you want it for the leaves, we like 'Santo', as it's slower to bolt. If you want coriander, consider the 'Delfino' variety, as it produces seeds more quickly.

PRESERVATION

Cilantro can be preserved by freezing, freeze-drying, or traditional drying.

We only preserve cilantro because we can't grow it and have ripe tomatoes at the same time in our climate. We love its taste in our salsa, so if we want to make salsa or any tomato-based dish that calls for cilantro, we have to preserve it for use later in the season. We preserve 1 to 2 pints (192 to 384 g) of freeze-dried cilantro from the volunteer plants that pop up in our raised beds each year. Freeze-dried cilantro is easy to use, being shelf stable, but you can also throw it in a zipper-sealed plastic bag and keep it in the freezer.

As with many aspects of the preserver's garden, it helps to think ahead. Even if you don't use something year-round, it's nice to have it when you need it.

CHIVES

If you're patient, this perennial herb will spread over time, providing plenty of chives during the growing season. We have a patch of chives about 4 square feet (0.4 sq m) in size. We can harvest them three or four times in the spring and early summer, giving us 1 to 2 pints (6 to 13 g) of dried chives in addition to plenty for fresh eating.

PLANNING CONSIDERATIONS: Chives belong to the onion family and have a mild, onion-like flavor. Chives can be grown from seed or purchased in root clumps, much like onion starts. They bloom the second year after planting and, if the flowers are left to mature, they can spread from the seeds and the roots. Both the leaves and flowers are edible. They're easy to dig up and transplant if they get out of hand and, best of all, once you plant them you typically don't have to plant them again. Remember where they are or mark them because you likely won't remember, and when they pop up in the spring they'll look a lot like grass.

SUN REQUIREMENT: Full sun.

GROWING SEASON: Spring and early summer.

HARVESTING: Cut off the flowers and leaves for fresh use or drying several times throughout the spring and early summer.

Chive flowers from our spring garden

VARIETIES WE LOVE

Garlic chives, classic chives, and Chinese chives are all great options.

PRESERVATION

Chives can be preserved by drying, freezing, or freeze-drying. We grow them to freeze-dry, as this maintains more flavor than other methods. We store the chives in half-pint (237 ml) jars with the rest of our herbs.

We use chives in our ranch seasoning mix, which can be mixed with sour cream, yogurt, or even mayonnaise to make homemade ranch dressing (see the parsley section on page 121 for the recipe).

We also love to have chives on hand to add to stir-fry dishes and fried rice.

PARSLEY

Bundles of fresh parsley hanging with other herbs to dry

Parsley is a biennial, meaning it grows leaves the first year and then comes back and blooms the second year. When growing parsley as an herb, it's often grown as an annual. It will continue to grow back after the leaves are cut all summer and into fall.

PLANNING CONSIDERATIONS: Parsley is easy to start from seed and transplant into your garden. Or you can purchase transplants from a nursery. We usually grow it as an annual for preservation since it will produce high-quality leaves the first year, is easily started from seed in the late winter, and survives into the late fall, even through a number of frosts and freezes.

We grow ten to twelve plants each year. When we tried to grow more than that, the plants produced an insane amount of leaves, which forced us to the realization that we just don't like parsley that much. The plants we have give us enough to dry or freeze-dry over 2 quarts (768 g) of parsley. If you're not a big parsley fan, don't grow so much.

SUN REQUIREMENT: Full sun to partial shade.

GROWING SEASON: Spring through fall.

HARVESTING: Remove the leaves as needed for fresh eating, or harvest entire stems by cutting them off at the base of the plant when you need more for preservation efforts.

VARIETIES WE LOVE

We like 'Triple Curled' parsley because it's hardier than other types we've tried, both in the thickness of its leaves and in its cold tolerance. Most parsley is a biannual and blooms in the second year.

PRESERVATION

Parsley is a popular herb that is widely used in cooking. It has a fresh, slightly bitter taste and is often used as a garnish or flavor enhancer in a variety of dishes.

Even with it being a key ingredient in our favorite ranch seasoning mix, we tend to have extra parsley each year, both fresh and preserved. Extra dried or fresh parsley makes a great treat for rabbits, chickens, and other animals around the homestead.

One of our favorite uses for preserved parsley is as a key ingredient in our homemade dairy-free ranch dressing powder. We use this powder as a salad dressing, a marinade, and more. We also make parsley salt, using the same method as we do for basil salt (described on page 113); we add it to our other salt blends and use it in soups.

RANCH SEASONING

FOR RANCH SEASONING MIX

½ cup (56 g) onion powder

½ cup (24 g) dried chives

½ cup (10 g) dried parsley

¼ cup (12 g) dried dill leaves

¼ cup (32 g) garlic powder

2 teaspoons ground black pepper

2 teaspoons salt

¼ cup (31 g) raw sugar (optional)

INSTRUCTIONS

Put all ingredients into your blender and grind to a consistent powder. Store in an airtight container until you're ready to use it. We store ours in a pint or half-pint Mason jar.

FOR RANCH DRESSING

½ cup (115 g) mayonnaise

¼ cup (60 ml) milk of your choice (we usually use coconut or almond, but cow milk works too!)

1 to 1½ tablespoons (6.3 to 9.5 g) Ranch Seasoning Mix (see above)

½ teaspoon basil or other herb salt (or regular salt)

INSTRUCTIONS

Blend or stir thoroughly, then let the mixture sit in the fridge overnight for the best flavor!

OREGANO

Oregano is a perennial herb that's easy to grow from seed and will also come back easily each year in moderate climates (it also survives well below freezing, with foliage surviving down to single-digit Fahrenheit/subzero Celsius temperatures). It spreads from runners under the soil but can be contained by trimming or pulling the runners where you don't want it to grow (unlike its cousin, mint). If you truly want to contain oregano, plant it in a container. When you pull up the runners, you can put them in pots to root and share oregano with your friends!

PLANNING CONSIDERATIONS: We like to preserve 2 to 3 quarts (768 g to 1.2 kg) of oregano per year. We have around three perennial oregano patches at any given time. There are usually enough leaves to harvest from the plants from April to November here in the Midwestern United States, so we only need to preserve enough for five months of the year–that is, if you don't mind the herb's flavor after it blooms. Personally, we don't notice a difference in the flavor of oregano after it flowers, but blooms can make the leaves look less pretty.

Dried oregano ready for winter use

SUN REQUIREMENT: Full sun.

GROWING SEASON: Spring through fall.

HARVESTING: Cut fresh stems off the plant, removing the amount you want. The plant will readily regrow and produce more stems for future harvests.

VARIETIES WE LOVE

We like both *Origanum vulgare* and marjoram oregano. *O. vulgare* is a versatile herb used in Italian cuisine. A hardy perennial herb, marjoram is native to southern Europe and has a milder, more delicate flavor. Both are good and bring their own qualities to recipes.

PRESERVATION

We use oregano to make oregano salt, or add it freshly chopped or dried and crushed to nearly any savory dish. It can be air-dried, dehydrated at a low temperature, freeze-dried, or frozen. Whether freeze-dried or air-dried, once dry the leaves will easily come off the woody stems. We prefer to dry oregano before breaking the leaves off the stems to store.

When freeze-drying oregano (as with basil, thyme, dill, and many other herbs), put whole stems into the freeze-dryer. After they're dry, press down on the tray of dried herbs with your palm; the leaves will break off and the stems will float to the top. The stems can then be picked out without having to take all those tiny leaves off each stem before freeze-drying. This saves time, but it also takes up more space in the freeze-dryer.

If you want to fit the most herbs possible into your freeze-dryer, you can pull the individual leaves off the stems before drying, blend them into a paste, and then freeze-dry that. This can then be broken up or blended again to make an herb powder.

THYME

We always need more thyme. But seriously: this is the one herb we never seem to have enough of.

PLANNING CONSIDERATIONS: Thyme is a perennial herb that can be grown from seed or cuttings. Thyme does not like to be too wet, so keep that in mind when choosing a planting location. We know as gardeners you may get tired of hearing that nearly everything wants well-drained soil, but for thyme, it really can mean the difference between a perennial herb and something that grows for a few months and then dies.

We'd love to tell you how much thyme to grow to preserve, but we haven't quite figured this one out. In our climate, we've had creeping thyme that keeps its leaves year-round, so we can harvest it whenever we need and have no reason to preserve it. This isn't always the case, and some years the plant dies back completely and we're left empty handed.

SUN REQUIREMENT: Full sun.

GROWING SEASON: Year-round in warmer climates; spring through fall in colder climates.

HARVESTING: For preserving large harvests, cut whole branches off of your thyme plant, ideally before it flowers. Small harvests can take place year-round. Don't expect a huge harvest. The tiny narrow leaves are difficult to remove efficiently, and we're lucky to get one-quarter cup (10 g) preserved from four to six plants.

VARIETIES WE LOVE

Choose the type of thyme you grow according to the size of your growing area. Wild, or creeping, thyme will grow outward like a carpet and will come back year after year—you can even walk on it without harming the plant. Other varieties grow more like a bush. Depending on your growing conditions, wild/creeping thyme can be rather aggressive, but like oregano it isn't difficult to contain by trimming or pulling runners.

PRESERVATION

Thyme can be dehydrated, air-dried, or freeze-dried. We love thyme on chicken. A favorite pairing in our house is chicken, garlic, and thyme. There are always recipes calling for thyme, but in general we go through it on chicken dishes. In the garlic profile below, we've included a chicken recipe that features thyme.

SAGE

Sage is easily grown from seeds or cuttings. This perennial herb will come back each year as long as it is well established before winter. This easy-to-grow herb will bloom the second year after planting and beyond. The blooms attract many kinds of pollinators and don't dramatically change the taste of the leaves. As a drought-tolerant plant, sage doesn't require much water, and it does well in the ground or in containers. It is deer resistant and may even repel deer if planted among other vegetables or flowers.

BREAKFAST SAUSAGE

Our favorite recipe for using dried sage is this breakfast sausage seasoning.

INGREDIENTS

2 pounds (907 g) ground pork (or beef, or half of each meat, depending on what you have)

2 teaspoons dry sage

1 teaspoon ground black pepper

2 teaspoons salt

1 tablespoon (15 g) brown sugar

½ teaspoon oregano

Pinch of ground cloves

Pinch of crushed red pepper (optional)

INSTRUCTIONS

Mix meat and spices thoroughly. Let sit in the refrigerator for at least an hour to let flavors combine. Press into patties or cook ground. Keep refrigerated until ready to use.

PLANNING CONSIDERATIONS: Eight to ten sage plants in a 3 x 3-foot (91 x 91 cm) bed will spread and give you enough sage to preserve 1 or 2 quarts (460 to 922 g) or more of died sage per year. To keep your harvest productive, either replant every three or four years, or be sure to stay on top of pruning and add compost or manure around the base of the plants each year. If left neglected, the plants may be smothered out by dead old growth and may tend to grow taller with fewer leaves.

SUN REQUIREMENT: Full sun.

GROWING SEASON: Year-round.

HARVESTING: Harvest individual leaves by cutting them from the stems at any time. Harvest whole stems for drying before the plants go to flower.

VARIETIES WE LOVE

We grow broadleaf sage. It seems to grow the best for us and is the easiest to harvest and dry.

PRESERVATION

Preserve sage like most other herbs: by drying or freeze-drying. We like to freeze-dry this herb, as it saves more of the flavor, color, and essential oils, but it's forgiving if you just air-dry it.

Sage is often sold as a powder, so if you'd like it to have the taste and texture of what you usually have in a commercial spice jar, blend dried sage into a powder.

A WORD ABOUT MINT IN THE PRESERVER'S GARDEN

Mint is the plant that can make any gardener feel successful. It can be grown from seed or cuttings, and is so easy to grow that, in the right growing conditions, it's considered invasive. Mint is a perennial that will spread continually if left unchecked. If this is a concern, we recommend growing it in a basket or an enclosed bed to prevent overspreading. Mint can often jump out of containers and invade other flower beds. If it escapes into your lawn, it will usually stop when it reaches an area that's mowed regularly. Our mint grows in concrete beds by our porch. We let it take over, as it's said that mint helps keep mice and other pests away from your house.

Our primary reason for growing mint is to keep mint extract on hand to flavor winter baked goods. To make mint extract, add fresh mint sprigs to a canning jar (about three-quarters full, loosely packed) and fill it with a clear alcohol of your choice. You can use pure cooking alcohol like Everclear, but we typically use vodka (the cheap stuff is okay). Vodka evaporates less quickly and is much less expensive. Let it sit in a cool, dry place for six to eight weeks and check the flavor. If it's strong enough for you, strain out the leaves and store the liquid for later use in recipes. Mint can also be dried or freeze-dried, or even frozen for tea or other uses.

→ One of our sage plants at peak summer flowering

GARLIC

How much garlic you should grow depends entirely on how much you eat. If you're like us and use a head of garlic when a recipe calls for a clove, 200 to 250 heads is a good number for a year. We arrived at this number because over 300 heads is hard to manage, but growing a little less gives us enough to preserve—some freeze-dried, some as garlic salt, and some to eat fresh. It's really not too much garlic for a family like ours, and if you really love garlic and have the time to plant, harvest, cure, and preserve some of it, you may want even more.

PLANNING CONSIDERATIONS: Garlic is easy to grow, it just takes some patience. To grow a head of garlic you need to plant a single garlic clove. You can order seed garlic, you can save your own, or you can even grow organic garlic from the produce section of the grocery store. You should try seed garlic, though, because operations that sell it take measures to ensure their cloves are free of disease.

We've done all of the above, and we've never had an issue with any garlic disease in our area. Seed garlic is quite expensive, so if you want to get started and don't want to spend a lot of money, just buy some organic garlic from the store and plant it. The conventionally grown (non-organic) garlic you find in the store is imported from overseas. We try to avoid garlic grown so far away, since it may have been grown without proper regulations and oversight, and also because of the distance it has traveled and the impact on the environment.

Garlic cloves need to be planted about 6 inches (15 cm) apart and 3 inches (7.5 cm) deep in the

↑ Harvested garlic plants curing with onions

← Several hundred garlic plants can fit in a relatively small space.

→ Garlic cloves separated and ready for planting in the garden

fall, when the soil temperature reaches about 50°F (10°C). In southern Missouri, with an early frost date in mid-October, that usually means we plant garlic in late October or early November. The plants will sprout in the fall but are quite hardy and will really start to grow when spring comes around. Garlic can be planted deeper in colder climates, and 4 to 6 inches (10 to 15 cm) of mulch can help keep it warm. Just don't overdo it: if you don't need that extra soil and mulch, don't waste your energy—and the plant's—by making it harder for the garlic to grow up through the soil.

SUN REQUIREMENT: Full sun.

GROWING SEASON: Garlic is planted in the fall and harvested the following summer.

HARVESTING: Harvest by loosening the soil and digging up the bulbs in late spring or early summer when the bottom two to four sets of leaves on the plant turn brown. When thinking about preserving your garlic, remember that it's important to dig it up and not pull your garlic as you would onions: this can damage the outside of the bulb and lessen its shelf life. Garlic should be harvested on a relatively dry day, not when the soil is soggy and wet. Dry the harvested heads of garlic outside in a warm space with good airflow, and away from direct sunlight, for a few weeks before storing.

VARIETIES WE LOVE

While there are many varieties of garlic to choose from, be aware of two important types: hardneck and softneck. Hardneck is more suited to colder climates, while softneck prefers warmer weather.

While similar in flavor, softneck garlic tends to have a longer pantry life. Besides not having a "hard neck" or stem, softneck garlic does not have a stalk coming up in the middle—the cloves are all shoved together and can be many different sizes. Hardneck garlic tends to have cloves of a similar size and shape that surround a hard stalk.

Despite the tendency of the hardneck variety to produce fewer cloves and smaller bulbs, about half the garlic we plant is of this type. That's because hardneck garlic produces garlic scapes, which we love to eat fresh, in stir-fries, and freeze-dried for later. Having at least one hundred garlic scapes gives us plenty of extra garlic flavor to make up for what the hardnecks may lack in the number of cloves we get from them. We also plant hardnecks to ensure success with our harvest, since our winters could theoretically kill off the softneck varieties (though this has never happened before).

Garlic offers many health benefits: it's high in antioxidants, anticarcinogenic, can boost immunity, and works as an anti-inflammatory. These qualities are enhanced the fresher your garlic is. Take cured or dried softneck garlic and braid it for storage, as overprocessing can also degrade those benefits. Garlic preservation may not be an issue, as softneck garlic can be stored for six to nine months.

PRESERVATION

For seasoning and cooking, store garlic for an extended period by freezing or drying it. Drying garlic in a dehydrator will forever scent your plastic dehydrator, so be sure your dehydrator is stainless steel. If you have a plastic dehydrator and plan on doing a lot of dehydrating, it's best to have one designated for garlic and onions. To freeze, remove the skins from the cloves and place them in an airtight container. You can also freeze garlic in a bit of water in ice-cube trays for later use.

← Garlic scapes are a delicious and underappreciated part of the garlic plant.

GARLIC CHICKEN

INGREDIENTS

1 whole chicken, cut into 8 pieces

10 to 15 sprigs thyme (use less if fresh, more if dried)

60 cloves garlic, peeled (I've been known to use more than 80)

¾ cup (178 ml) olive oil

Salt and pepper to taste

INSTRUCTIONS

Add 2 tablespoons (30 ml) of the olive oil to an oven-safe pan (we love cast-iron pans for this recipe) and put on the stovetop on medium heat.

Season chicken with salt and pepper, add to pan and brown on all sides.

Turn off heat, add remainder of oil. Scatter the garlic cloves and thyme sprigs evenly throughout the pan, making sure they are covered in oil.

Move to a 350°F (180°C) oven and bake for around 90 minutes.

Enjoy the chicken, but the real star of the show is the garlic and oil that's left over. It can be stored and used as a spread on bread or biscuits.

You can also use your harvest to make garlic oil. Heat the base oil of your choice in a pan until near its typical cooking temperature, then add crushed garlic. Cook until the garlic browns. Strain out the garlic and use the oil in recipes and as a cooking oil within two weeks or freeze it.

We also like to make roasted garlic in large batches in a slow cooker by cooking the garlic in oil until somewhat caramelized, then freezing in small portions to add to dishes and sauces later. Either roasted garlic or garlic oil can be frozen in ice-cube trays and then transferred to an airtight, freezer-safe container for storage.

CARROTS

We always like to have carrots on hand. They're easy to grow in the spring and fall successions (note that they don't like summer heat), and they can be preserved via a number of methods.

PLANNING CONSIDERATIONS: Directly sow the seeds on the surface of smooth, loose soil. The seeds need to be kept damp and dark for good germination. You can use cardboard to protect the seeds from sunlight and to keep the soil moist, but check under it daily and remove it promptly when they sprout.

Carrots need loose soil without many rocks. Make sure to match the projected length of your carrots, listed on the seed packet to the depth of your workable, loose soil.

Carrots grow well in containers and are cold tolerant. Frost on fall-growing carrots makes them sweeter.

SUN REQUIREMENT: Full to partial sun; shade on summer afternoons.

GROWING SEASON: Spring and fall (they don't like summer's heat).

PESTS: If you notice root damage on your carrots when harvesting, the most likely pests are carrot flies or carrot weevils. We've had minor issues with both, though we've never truly identified which species is causing the problems. We avoid these pests by planting our carrots in fresh soil contained in raised beds, rotating where they're planted every year or two. Neem oil and row

← Freshly harvested carrots, washed and ready to be preserved

covers can also help if you're struggling with root damage on your carrot crops.

Carrot seedlings are most vulnerable to damage from slugs and snails. While aphids, cutworms, flea beetles, and cabbage loppers can also damage carrots, we haven't had major issues with pests on carrots in the summer.

As mentioned in the dill profile, black swallowtail caterpillars like to munch on carrot greens. If your carrots are small when these caterpillars arrive, you may need to relocate the little critters to dill, parsley, or wild carrot (Queen Anne's lace) if available. If you have abundant greens on your carrots, letting the caterpillars stay won't do much damage.

HARVESTING: Gently dig or pull carrots from the ground when they reach the days to maturity noted on the seed packet, or when their shoulders are around the diameter of a United States quarter. Digging after rain makes the job easier.

VARIETIES WE LOVE

For canning and storage, we like 'Red Store' Chantenay, 'Danvers 126', and 'Danvers Half Long'. These last are especially good if you have rocky soil or shallow raised beds.

For fresh eating, we tend to gravitate toward more boldly colored carrots like 'Cosmic Purple', 'Atomic Red', and 'Parisian'. Nantes carrots have limited storage potential compared to other varieties, while Chantenay carrots have greater storage potential. When you read about a carrot variety it will tell you the potential and average length of the carrot; be sure your loose, rock-free soil is deep enough to support that length.

PRESERVING

Pressure canning, freezing, and freeze-drying are great ways to preserve carrots. There are pros and cons to each method, of course. Pressure-canned carrots are softer, and freeze-dried carrots need to be kept in complete darkness until you're ready to use them or they'll fade to white, which is unappealing and a potential sign they've lost some nutritional value. Mylar bags are the best way to store freeze-dried carrots.

You need about 18 pounds (8 kg) of carrots for a canner-load of 7 quarts (3 kg) or 11 pounds (5 kg) for 9 pints (2 kg).

Carrots also last a long time in cold storage. We clean our carrots and put them in the refrigerator in a plastic bag (otherwise they dry out and get rubbery). Since we don't typically grow enough for our family for a full year, we eat carrots through the spring, summer, fall, and a little bit into winter, then take a few months off. If we ever get a huge crop of carrots, we freeze-dry them. When prepared this way, our kids love to eat them as a crunchy snack—either plain or as a delivery mechanism for hummus.

Organically grown bulk carrots are easily accessible in most areas if you want to pressure-can carrots or need to add some store-bought ones to your harvest to make preservation worth it—but with some planning you can store carrots to enjoy fresh for most of the year.

A fresh carrot harvest awaits storage and preservation

BROCCOLI/CAULIFLOWER

Broccoli and cauliflower plants should be spaced at 12 to 18 inches (30 to 46 cm) apart, depending on how big you expect the plants to get. Most guides say 18 inches (46 cm), but realistically we do fine with 12-inch (30 cm) spacing.

PLANNING CONSIDERATIONS: Classified as cole crops, otherwise known as brassicas, broccoli and cauliflower are cool-season vegetables that grow best in temperatures between 60°F and 68°F (16°C and 20°C). They don't mind a bit of frost, but if it's going to dip below 30°F (–1°C), we always recommend covering them with a sheet or frost cloth. If you wait until too late in the spring to plant, high temperatures (over 78°F [26°C]) will generally shut the plants down and you won't get much of a harvest. We've also had good luck in our climate—where we go from the last frost to 80-degree (27°C) days in a couple weeks or less—with sprouting broccoli (or Chinese broccoli). Broccoli is an excellent alternative for places with warmer weather or springs with wild temperature variations.

SUN REQUIREMENT: Full to partial sun.

GROWING SEASON: Spring: These crops can also be started in the summer indoors for fall harvests.

↑ Broccoli florets ready to be freeze-dried

← Freeze-dried broccoli florets on the shelf

PESTS: Brassicas as a whole share many common pests, though some prefer certain brassicas over others. Cabbage worms, cabbage loppers, cross-striped cabbage worms, and diamondback moth caterpillars are typically the worst pests in the early season for these crops. Since none of these requires pollination for the vegetable to be harvested, row covers can be helpful for preventing airborne threats, including the adult forms of these pests. *Bacillus thuringiensis* (Bt) is the active ingredient in many organic caterpillar sprays; it's a good control option, since at times the row covers can be hard to deal with due to wind or when trying to harvest. When applied weekly, Bt has been very successful on our farm against cabbage worms.

Slugs and snails can also become a problem with young seedlings. Later in the summer, harlequin beetles become a concern when growing crops like broccoli, cauliflower, Brussels sprouts, and kale. They're less of a concern with cabbage because you harvest it before the harlequin beetle season really begins (later in summer). To combat these pests, we've had to stop leaving our brassicas in the garden over the summer, instead taking them out and feeding them to the chickens when they're past their prime. Like other beetles, harlequin beetles are difficult to eradicate using organic methods. Handpicking and removing eggs is our primary defense while we're still harvesting.

HARVESTING: Use a sharp knife to cut broccoli heads from the plants before the flowers open. For cauliflower, cut off the heads while the curds are still tight. Covering the heads by folding the leaves closed and fastening them shut with a clothespin will blanch the growing cauliflower and keep it bright white. And don't forget to pick the side shoots that develop after the main head of broccoli has been harvested: these can be great thrown into a stir-fry.

VARIETIES WE LOVE

Our go-to variety of broccoli is 'Destiny Hybrid'. It does well in warmer climates and is later to bolt. In cooler climates, broccoli is easier to grow and more varieties will thrive.

When it comes to cauliflower, a large white variety called 'Amazing' is what we've had the best luck with. Cauliflower is even more prone to bolting in the heat than broccoli, so consider the length of your spring growing season and choose a faster maturing variety if you're in a warmer climate.

PRESERVATION

Broccoli and cauliflower can be frozen with good effect, but both must be blanched in boiling water for two to three minutes before dunking them in ice water to quickly cool. For best results, vacuum-seal before freezing, as they are subject to freezer burn. These two vegetables also freeze-dry well, but they can be delicate and prone to crushing.

Don't forget the leaves—broccoli and cauliflower leaves are a crop all their own (see spinach and other greens on the next page for preservation methods).

SPINACH, KALE & OTHER GREENS

As baby greens, these crops can be grown in a small space. On a larger scale, space apart spinach 6 inches (15 cm), kale 9 inches (23 cm), and collard greens 12 inches (30 cm). Greens can also be grown between or around other plants. Spinach stays relatively short, so it can be grown easily around taller plants, or where taller plants will come up later in the season, like cucumbers, pole beans, and peas.

PLANNING CONSIDERATIONS: Consider succession planting by planting greens in spring and then following them with something that prefers warmer temperatures in the summer. Many greens tend to bolt when temperatures get above 80°F (27°C). You can provide shade either by planting them in a space that gets afternoon shade or by using shade cloth to help keep them from bolting too soon.

As always, how much you plant for preservation will depend on your family and the amount you want to eat during the time when greens

are not available fresh from your garden. One measurement to keep in mind: it takes about 28 pounds (13 kg) of greens to fill seven quart (946 ml) jars for a full pressure canner load. If you expect to eat a quart (170 g) of greens a week with your meals, make sure you grow and preserve a *lot* of greens.

SUN REQUIREMENTS: Full sun in early spring, shade later in the season.

GROWING SEASON: Spring and fall; most greens dislike the heat of summer.

PESTS: Aphids are our biggest pest concern for spinach and other greens that aren't kale (see the pest information for other brassicas, such as cabbage or broccoli), with slugs coming in second. Combatting slugs in the garden during the cooler, wetter spring months can be a full-time job. Consider setting beer traps (shallow saucers filled with beer) when you plant your greens if you believe you have an issue with slugs and snails.

While decomposer insects serve an important role in the garden, if they get out of hand they can be very destructive. Roly polys (pillbugs) are normally decomposers, munching on dead leaves, but they become a common pest for us, especially in raised beds. When trapped in a small space, a raised bed, or even in a garden with a lot of decomposing material, they tend to overpopulate and will eat your young plants. They fall into beer traps made for slugs, making management easy. Earwigs can also be destructive decomposers. They can be trapped by laying pieces of corrugated cardboard in the garden. Earwigs crawl into the cardboard's tunnels during the day where they can then be knocked out into a jar of soapy water.

HARVESTING: Greens can be cut again and again, as long as you leave the growing tip at the top of the plant intact (in some cases you can even cut the tip and it will branch, but they'll take longer to regrow).

↑ A mixed green salad, fresh out of the garden

← A row of kale plants in our spring garden

VARIETIES WE LOVE

Kale: Dinosaur kale, 'Dazzling Blue' kale

'Dwarf Blue Curled' kale for kale chips (though pests can hide in the frilly leaves)

These three varieties have fewer issues with pests when planted with 'Red Russian' kale, which pests tend to prefer, so we plant a few of them on the end of the row to draw the pests away from the other varieties.

'Space' (a hybrid) and 'Bloomsdale Long Standing' (an heirloom) are our favorite spinach varieties.

PRESERVATION

When most people think of greens, they think of salads or canned spinach like Popeye eats. While we love baby spinach salad with fresh strawberries, spinach has many more uses.

You may not have thought to preserve greens for your food storage, especially if your family doesn't like soggy canned greens.

In our house, we use powders from dried spinach and other leafy greens to sneak more nutrients into otherwise less nutritious foods.

EXTENDING THE FRESH GREENS HARVEST

The time of year when you *can't* grow fresh greens in most climates is relatively short. There are even ways to grow fresh greens indoors with grow lights and outdoors in a cold frame or hoop house for much of the winter. Our kale and other cold-hardy greens barely stay alive in our cold frame during the coldest two months, when the daylight dwindles to less than ten hours a day. Even if it isn't too cold, the plants will still go dormant and pause their growth. If your greens are a harvestable size before this happens and you can protect them from the cold to prevent them from being damaged, you can continue to harvest fresh greens through the winter in many climates. We have had kale overwinter in our cold frame even with temperatures dipping to just below freezing (0°C). If it gets even colder, we take additional measures to protect our plants. As noted, growth is slowed dramatically when daylight hours go below ten hours a day.

COLD FRAMES

Cold frames are essentially miniature, ground-level greenhouses used for extending the growing season for smaller crops. We typically use ours for greens. We built a small cold frame on the south side of one of our greenhouses. It has a clear plastic cover angled to catch maximum heat from the winter sun.

A note about cold frame growing: if you plant your cold frame too late in the season, your veggies will appear to grow, but you'll basically be growing miniature versions. This is due to the lack of sunlight in the winter. We've grown lots of tiny greens, tiny radishes, and tiny carrots in an effort to get this timing right.

For example, when we make fresh fruit smoothies, we always include some spinach or kale powder to add a boost of vitamin A, vitamin C, and iron. Making your own greens powders can add nutritional value to your food and save you money. Look up the cost of greens powders—they're not cheap—and growing your own makes a lot of sense. As a family of eight, three to four quart (946 ml) jars of greens powder are usually enough for adding to smoothies, scrambled eggs, and baked goods to get us through the seasons when fresh greens aren't available (for us that's November through March). With a cold frame or a low tunnel, we can extend the season for fresh greens by a couple of extra months.

To make greens powder, blend the leaves then dehydrate or freeze-dry to turn them into a powder. See a photo of kale powder right out of the freeze-dryer on page 81.

Unlike spinach and kale, lettuce and other watery, light greens don't make quality greens powder that tastes good. To make the process more effective, we grow our preserving greens and our salad greens separately, even though we will eat some of the preservable greens on salads. As all the greens start to mature, having them separate is easier when we harvest them for preservation.

You can also preserve greens like spinach and kale by freeze-drying, where the whole leaves can be added to soups and casseroles year-round and offer the texture you get from fresh greens. Kale can also be freeze-dried or dehydrated to make kale chips.

You can also blanch and then freeze spinach and kale in vacuum bags for later cooking.

Pressure-canned spinach (or any greens, for that matter) aren't for everyone, but this is another way to preserve your harvest. Fitting canned spinach into your diet might work for you if you enjoy the flavor and texture of cooked greens. We need to be creative with our preserved greens, as they aren't typically something our family enjoys.

SWEET POTATOES (YAMS)

If you've never grown sweet potatoes, you may not know that they are a completely different type of plant and completely unrelated to standard potatoes. They're a vining plant that loves warm to hot conditions and typically needs a much longer season to grow. Most sweet potatoes take on average 100 to 150 days to mature (if you're careful in selecting varieties, though, you can find some that will mature in a shorter period of time). To maximize your sweet potato harvest, prune vines to 3 to 4 feet (91 to 122 cm) from their roots to allow the plant to focus on growing roots. If you live somewhere with a shorter growing season, you can start them in a greenhouse or indoors.

Sweet potatoes make great houseplants and will grow in water. Once you put them in dirt they'll start making roots and will create clusters of sweet potatoes once planted out.

PLANNING CONSIDERATIONS: Grow five to ten sweet potato plants for each person who eats them in your family. We grow as many as we can fit in the containers and raised beds around our garden. We plant sweet potatoes not only in our garden beds but also in our decorative flower beds. Raised beds and containers make the sweet potatoes easier to harvest and they don't seem to mind growing in this manner.

This past year, we planted sweet potatoes all over the garden and throughout the landscaping. Their vines pouring out of the raised beds provided not only beauty but a bit of cover to help suppress weed growth. As a result, we harvested 80 pounds (36 kg) of sweet potatoes at the end of the season. It was a good year for sweet potatoes. We had something like thirty plants in total, but we still enjoyed a great yield.

SUN REQUIREMENT: These plants prefer full sun and love heat.

GROWING SEASON: Summer; the vines are readily killed by frost.

PESTS: We don't have an issue with pests on sweet potatoes, though occasionally we'll have a few holes in the leaves. Deer and other wildlife love sweet potatoes, so you may need to protect their foliage from these critters. As with other crops, planting them in soil that's warm enough (you want a soil temperature of at least 60°F [16°C]) will help them be healthier and resist pests.

HARVESTING: Harvest immediately before the first frost, as frost will kill the vines and damage the sweet potatoes. If you live in an area with late frosts or no frosts at all, harvest when the leaves begin to yellow, indicating that the roots are mature.

To get a large harvest it's essential to give your plants a long enough season to grow. We start sweet potatoes by growing our own slips (rooted sweet potato shoots) indoors or in our greenhouse, keeping them at a minimum of 75°F (24°C) from mid-March until it's time to plant out in mid-May—that is, a few weeks after your last frost, when the soil temps have warmed a bit and the overnight lows won't dip below 50°F (10°C) . They're typically harvested by mid-October, giving them five full months of growing time in the garden, plus an extra two months of growing as a slip.

Sweet potatoes must be cured before storage. Store newly unearthed sweet potatoes in a warm, humid environment for about a week—around 85°F (29°C) and 90 percent humidity is ideal. During this time, dents, cuts, and other imperfections will heal over, and they'll develop their sweetness. They can then be stored in a typical cellar environment with 50 to 60 percent humidity.

VARIETIES WE LOVE

Choose the varieties you grow based on your location. If you're new to growing sweet potatoes, find a local farmer or gardener willing to sell or give you slips, then you can save potatoes from that first crop and grow your own slips the next year. Buying local will help you get the best variety for your area.

PRESERVATION

Sweet potato storage is preferred over preservation in many cases, as the potatoes will last months after curing without further preparation.

Just remember that you need to cure the tubers in order to achieve the best flavor and storage life.

Sweet potatoes can be preserved via our normal methods, but we only preserve them in the ways we prefer to eat them as a bonus to having them fresh.

FREEZE-DRYING: Freeze-drying sweet potatoes is easy. They can be raw or cooked, depending on your preference. Cooked sweet potatoes may be easier to rehydrate, but this can also be done with raw sweet potatoes. Be aware that, if you don't fully rehydrate them before cooking, they'll be rubbery or gummy. We generally peel the sweet potatoes and cut into ½ inch (1 cm) cubes.

PRESSURE CANNING: Sweet potatoes can be pressure canned in chunks in water or syrup, if you like them sweeter. This makes a product similar to buying sweet potatoes in a can. They're convenient for recipes in a way similar to canned white potatoes.

You'll need about 2 pounds (907 g) of sweet potatoes per quart (946 ml) jar for canning, or 1 pound per pint jar (454 g per 473 ml). When you think about it that way, we could have 1 quart (784 g) a week through the year with only 100 pounds (45 kg) of sweet potatoes. Sweet potatoes can be raw packed.

DEHYDRATING: To dehydrate sweet potatoes, slice them with a mandolin (or a knife if you have a lot of time on your hands) to about ¼ inch (6 mm) thick. Once sliced, blanch for four to five minutes in boiling water. This will make crunchy sweet potatoes, but you can also rehydrate them into a casserole.

We also like dehydrated sweet potato shreds for making sweet potato hash browns. Shred, blanch for two or three minutes, and dehydrate.

In addition, you can make sweet potato flour by dehydrating mashed cooked sweet potatoes.

Starting Your Own Sweet Potato Slips

To start our own slips, we use organic store-bought or homegrown sweet potatoes. Place potatoes in a pan filled with sand mixed evenly with soil. The potatoes will be half under the soil, half above. Keep your soil moist but not wet. Place the potatoes in a spot where they get sun and stay above 75°F (24°C) all the time. We do this in our greenhouse, moving the sweet potato pans to a germination chamber overnight—they could also be placed in a warm sunny window, but it's important to recognize that, even if your house is 70°F (21°C), the soil temperature will be 10°F (6°C) cooler, which in this case would mean the potatoes might not get warm enough to sprout slips.

Another option would be to place sweet potatoes in a produce basket on your kitchen counter and tell everyone you're going to cook them—this can encourage them to sprout (ha ha). If you use the second method, be sure to move the potatoes to a sunny spot after sprouting so they won't stretch.

Once the slip is a few inches tall (ideally 2 to 3 inches [5 to 7.5 cm] at minimum), you can twist it off the potato and root it in 1 cup (237 ml) of water. We like to use old popsicle molds for rooting sweet potato slips, but any cup or container will do. You can also root them in moist soil, but be careful not to let it dry out. That is part of the benefit of making slips in the half soil-filled tray: often they'll root and sprout at the same time, so when you pull off a slip it will already have roots attached.

POTATOES

By far our favorite starch, potatoes are a staple in our kitchen. Since we can't grow rice (our second favorite starch) where we live, we grow a lot of potatoes and store them in a variety of ways. Fresh potatoes are the most versatile, but we also eat them canned, dehydrated, and freeze-dried throughout the year.

We plan to purchase our potatoes every year, beyond what we grow.

PLANNING CONSIDERATIONS: Each potato plant yields an average of around 3 to 5 pounds (1.4 to 2.2 kg). In a good year, we get 80 to 100 pounds (36 to 45 kg) of potatoes from three 30-foot (9 m) rows. We always find it challenging to grow enough potatoes for all our needs, so we tend to grow our own potatoes for eating during the summer months, then purchase bulk organic potatoes each month over the winter. Our family goes through 50 to 75 pounds (23 to 34 kg) of potatoes each month. Growing this amount would require producing over five times what we currently grow. We did try this once, but, with our rocky soil and watering challenges, it proved to be more work than it was worth. We don't purchase bulk potatoes every month, instead we purchase them periodically, augmenting our supply with preserved potatoes. When buying potatoes, we generally purchase about 25 percent more than what we can eat fresh and then can a batch or two for later use. This leaves us with convenient cooked potatoes on the shelf, which is nice when we run out of our fresh supply.

Potatoes prefer to be planted just before the last spring frost, but when they pop up and grow, their foliage is frost sensitive—so getting the timing right is important. Potatoes are planted

↑ One of our potato patches

← The beginning of potato harvesting

→ Freshly cut seed potatoes, ready to plant

from seed potatoes. These are potatoes that, if purchased from a seed company or local farm store, are grown for the purpose of growing more potatoes. Alternatively, they can be saved from your own previous potato crop.

Potatoes you want to use for seed can be stored underground. It's best to dig them up, choose the potatoes you'd like to keep for seed, then rebury them in a mound. This will keep them at the right temperature and the proper humidity. To prevent them from growing, keep the soil dry by placing a roof of thick hay on the mound.

When it's time to plant your potatoes, each seed potato can be cut up into several pieces. Each seed potato should have an eye to sprout and be large enough (about the side of a golf ball or a bit larger) so that it doesn't rot. Remember that the starch in a potato is the energy for the next plant to grow, so make sure to leave enough food for the plant to get started.

In most of the United States, local lore tells us to plant potatoes on St Patrick's Day (March 17). Though many people do this, and we did for years, it likely results in a smaller crop of potatoes. Potatoes won't grow until the soil warms a bit, so planting early is safe in that respect. When we plant potatoes in mid-March, we don't see growth above soil for three to four weeks. If you're in an area where spring temperatures fluctuate wildly, your newly sprouted potato plants may die back multiple times before they really get growing. This can result in smaller crops due to wasted energy.

To plant potatoes before your last frost—but safely—consider keeping a close eye on them. You can mulch or hill your potatoes when they start to sprout. Covering them with hay or straw can protect them from a light frost without sacrificing tradition.

There are many methods of growing potatoes, with many gardeners insisting that you must hill your potatoes for a bigger crop. In our personal experience this hasn't helped significantly, except in cases where the potatoes were planted on top of the soil and just buried in mulch, straw, or hay. Whether grown in potato towers, with hilling, or with trenching, always prune flowers off your potato plants so their energy will be directed into

the roots. It's also important to make sure potatoes have loose fertile soil to grow in. The main advantage to planting potatoes in hills or mounds is that it makes harvesting a little easier. When you are turning soil over to get the potatoes out of the ground, the mounds make it marginally easier.

Potatoes like a fair amount of water. We try to make sure they get about an inch (2.5 cm) of water per week, but more won't hurt them if they're in good soil. Since your goal is tubers, just make sure that you don't apply so much water that the potatoes rot. We've found that, as it relates to water, potatoes are forgiving, and unless there's an extreme drought they can be largely left alone.

SUN REQUIREMENT: Plant potatoes in full sun, with an optional bit of afternoon shade.

GROWING SEASON: Spring through fall; young foliage is frost sensitive.

PESTS: Colorado potato beetles are the biggest pest you'll find on your potatoes. We don't have much of an issue with them where we are, but if you do get them, food-grade diatomaceous earth powder is effective and completely safe for the potatoes. A better way to avoid potato beetles is to make sure you don't plant your potatoes too early—potatoes that are stressed and planted in soil that's too cold will be more susceptible to pests.

Pressure-canned potato chunks

HARVESTING: Potatoes are ready to harvest when the plants turn yellow and die back. Be sure to keep an eye on your plants, as this can happen quickly if the weather conditions are harsh. If you have weeds or have interplanted other crops, you may lose your potatoes when the tops die completely. They'll still be there, but if you don't know where to dig you may not find them again, a frustrating situation.

Storing potatoes is another reason we don't grow all we need for the year. The space it would take to store more than 600 pounds (272 kg) of potatoes for the year is daunting. Potatoes need to be cured before storage. To cure, leave them in a warm, dry place for seven to ten days to develop thicker skins and heal wounds. Potatoes stored below 50°F (10°C) will not cure. Growing storage varieties helps this process along, but any potato can benefit from curing before cold storage.

Avoid storing potatoes with onions, bananas, or apples, as these produce ethylene, which will case the potatoes to sprout earlier than they otherwise would. Make sure your potatoes are stored in such a way that you can easily check all the layers to make sure they aren't rotting. We store our cured potatoes in plastic milk crates, allowing for airflow and easy stacking.

VARIETIES WE LOVE

Best storage varieties:

- Russet
- 'Kennebec'

Generally, the whiter, starchier varieties will last the longest in your cellar.

Unique varieties:

- Fingerling types
- Purple or other uniquely colored potato varieties.

These are tasty and fun to prepare and eat, but usually have a shorter shelf life, and will not yield the 3 to 5 pounds (1.4 to 2.3 kg) per plant that more mainstream varieties can claim.

Best for canning:

- 'Yukon Gold'
- 'Red Gold'
- 'Red Bliss'

When canning, denser, waxy potatoes will stand up the best to the harsh conditions of a pressure canner. Starchier potatoes like russets are more fragile and will tend to dissolve more when canned.

PRESERVATION

Potatoes can be preserved several ways: As a general rule, potatoes always need to be blanched before preserving. When preserving dry (freezing, freeze-drying, dehydrating), this prevents discoloration. Potatoes that are dehydrated without blanching will turn dark brown to black; still edible, they'll look rather unappetizing. Before canning, blanching will reduce the starch somewhat, making the water less cloudy and gummy.

When considering how you want to preserve potatoes, think about how you like to eat them. If your family eats a lot of boiled potatoes, pressure canning may be a great storage method for you, providing ready-to-eat boiled potatoes. These can be drained and added to recipes that call for boiled potatoes, they can be mashed, or they can be drained and patted dry and fried up in a skillet.

Potatoes can also be frozen if prepared properly. Cut them into whatever shape you want to eat them (sliced, shredded, fries, chips), blanch in boiling water for two to three minutes, followed by an ice-water-bath, dry them, then freeze flat on a baking sheet. They can be stored in zipper-top or vacuum-sealed bags.

We don't freeze-dry potatoes much because other methods work so much better. Freeze-dried potatoes can take a long time to rehydrate; if you don't rehydrate them fully, the texture can be off-putting—leathery, gummy, or even chalky. If you want to freeze-dry potatoes, consider freeze-drying fully cooked mashed potatoes for a quick and better-than-store-bought instant mashed potato.

Dehydrating is much the same as freeze-drying. You can do it, just know that rehydrating takes a long time—and don't forget to blanch!

SMASHED HERB POTATOES

INGREDIENTS

Canned potato chunks
Olive oil
Herb salt
Garlic

INSTRUCTIONS

Drain your chunked potatoes and space them evenly on a baking sheet lined with parchment paper. Using the bottom of a Mason jar, press on each potato until it collapses (not too much pressure, just enough to flatten it a little).

Drizzle with olive oil, add herb salt and garlic to taste.

Bake in 400°F (200°C) oven until lightly browned.

CABBAGE

Cabbage is a cole crop, like broccoli and cauliflower. We eat and preserve cabbage completely differently than other cole crops, though: Since cabbage is an early spring plant, and we don't have a lot going on in our spring garden, we're able to grow a large amount of cabbage. A rule of thumb for starting out is to grow three to four plants per person in your family. This is about the amount of cabbage we grow, but we're eating that much cabbage year-round. Each cabbage plant grows one head of cabbage, so it can be easy to calculate if you know how many heads you'd like to grow per year.

PLANNING CONSIDERATIONS: How much cabbage you grow depends on how much you want to eat. We primarily grow green cabbage heads for sauerkraut and napa cabbage for kimchi. You'll need about 2 pounds (907 g) of cabbage (two to four heads, depending on how big you grow them) per quart (946 ml) jar of sauerkraut. It takes a similar amount of napa cabbage to make a comparable amount of kimchi. While this seems like a lot of cabbage to make a relatively small amount of finished product, remember that you're removing most of the water from the cabbage in this process. If you like to eat fresh cabbage, account for that as well.

SUN REQUIREMENT: Full sun.

GROWING SEASON: Spring and fall.

PESTS: See the profile section for broccoli/cauliflower for an overview of pests that attack cabbage and how to address them

← Cabbage is a staple crop in our preservation garden.

HARVESTING: Cut the head from the plant when it is firm and fully formed, but before it begins to crack.

VARIETIES WE LOVE

We grow two types of cabbage: head cabbage and napa.

For our head cabbage, we grow 'Dutch Flat' cabbage (a great heirloom variety) and 'Ruby Perfection'. They both grow well in our area and can usually produce before spring pests eat them all.

Our favorite Chinese cabbage variety came from a local Korean market—the packet was completely in Korean, with the exception of "kimchi cabbage" in English. We would encourage you to try to find a similar source for your Asian cabbage varieties.

PRESERVATION

We've experimented with freeze-drying cabbage, and it does work for soups and stews, but cabbage cannot be rehydrated to do much else. Freeze-dried cabbage is fragile, like other freeze-dried greens: if you love the flavor of cabbage in your favorite stew, this is a good way to get the taste, if not the texture.

Fermentation is the most common cabbage preservation method, as sauerkraut or kimchi (see our kimchi recipe on page 62.)

Cabbage cannot be canned safely. Other greens can be canned, so why not cabbage? The answer is, canned cabbage has never been tested. Canning cabbage intensifies the flavor and degrades the texture and color so much that it's been deemed inedible. The powers-that-be in the canning safety world have never expected anyone would want to eat it, so its safety has not been evaluated.

Cabbage can be stored in a root cellar at 90 percent humidity. Fall-grown cabbage can easily last through the entire winter in a root cellar, which is another reason canning cabbage never seemed worth trying.

Washing napa cabbage as we prepare to make kimchi.

PEAS

There are many varieties of peas with so many options available for the home gardener. They range from miniature dwarf varieties that grow to 12 to 14 inches (30 to 36 cm) in size, all the way to full-size varieties that grow to 5 to 7 feet (1.5 to 2 m) tall. Find something that will fit your space. If you want to have enough peas to preserve, know that you'll need to grow a lot of plants. Peas are efficient in terms of square footage, as they can be planted close together in rows on a trellis. We plant our peas 1 to 3 inches (2.5 to 7.5 cm) apart along a fence so they can climb. If you don't give your peas a trellis, they'll still grow, but harvesting will be more difficult, yields will be lower, and pest pressure will be higher. The ability to grow up enables them to get more sunlight and makes them much easier to harvest.

PLANNING CONSIDERATIONS: Peas are a great addition to the food preservation garden. Like beans, they're grown for their pods and for the peas inside. The most common types that people know are snap peas, snow peas, and shelling peas. Find out what kind of peas your family enjoys. We grow snap peas and snow peas almost exclusively and skip the shelling peas. When we evaluate the space taken up in the garden versus the amount of food we get into the pantry, snap peas have produced best for us. We love having snap peas to add to vegetable stir-fry dishes throughout the year. Regardless of the type, peas need a trellis to grow on.

Peas prefer cooler temperatures, below about 80°F (27°C), so the seeds should be planted in the very early spring. When temperatures are excessively warm and humid, we run into problems

↑ Sugar snap peas ready for the kitchen

← Early season peas growing on our tomato trellis

with our pea season being cut short. All parts of the pea plants are tasty and edible for humans, and many other creatures enjoy them as well.

In our garden, we used to grow twenty to forty pea plants each year, and we never could figure out why we didn't have enough for anything other than fresh eating. Then one year, we planted 300 pea plants. We planted about half of these early in the spring (around the same time as when we planted onions), transplanted them from our greenhouse, and added about the remaining 150 plants by direct-seeding them into the garden at the same time. This enabled us to get two successions in one planting. That year we put up over 50 quarts (26 kg) of freeze-dried snow peas. Last year we cut back to a more manageable 100 plants, concerned that we didn't have the space for so many again. We ended up not preserving much at all—only about 15 quarts (8 kg) (plus some for fresh eating). Now we know that, if we want to preserve peas, we need to go all out. Snow peas also require daily harvesting or they'll grow too large and lose their tenderness.

SUN REQUIREMENT: Full sun; can handle some shade in the summer.

GROWING SEASON: Early spring or fall.

PESTS: Aphids are the biggest pest we've dealt with when growing peas, with slugs being a close second. To combat aphids, a mild soapy water solution sprayed daily immediately upon the first sighting can help. Using anything harsher is not only unnecessary but can harm beneficial insects that consume aphids, like ladybugs and lacewing larvae. While some varieties seem to be more prone to aphid infestation, the weather also plays a role, with warm, humid springs leading to the most problems.

HARVESTING: Pick or cut peas from the vines when they're ripe. Snow peas are picked when the pods are flat, before the peas inside fully develop. Snap peas (also called sugar snaps) have edible pods that are harvested when the peas inside are mostly developed. Shell peas are harvested when the pods are thick and the peas inside fully formed. Don't wait too long to harvest shell peas, though, or the peas themselves will be tough.

VARIETIES WE LOVE

For snow peas, we like 'Oregon Giant', 'Oregon Sugar Pod II,' and 'Golden Sweet Pea'.

We also like 'Wando' pea (cold and heat tolerant), and 'Lincoln' pea (a great high-yielding heirloom) as shelling peas.

For snap peas, try 'Sugar Snap', which is a bit more heat tolerant than others, and 'Sugar Lace II'. They have small compact plants and tiny, but tasty, peas. They're very productive, don't require trellising, and are great as in-patio planters.

PRESERVATION

When considering pea preservation, it's important to understand the differences between varieties. While I enjoy eating all types of peas, snap peas are by far the better choice for freeze-drying. Because the peas are essentially little balls of moisture inside the pods, it can be difficult to freeze-dry pods with peas inside them. We want to put up fully dry pea pods, so I cut each pod into two or three pieces before putting them in the freeze-dryer.

Our second choice for preserving peas is to freeze them. Peas need to be blanched for about one minute before freezing. Use vacuum bags to further preserve them in the freezer.

It's also safe to pressure-can peas and snap and snow peas. Canned shelling peas doesn't have the best reputation, but if they're anything like other home-canned foods, they'll taste better just because you made them at home.

↖ Peas about to be freeze-dried

↑ Peas just coming out of the freeze-dryer

↓ Jar of freeze-dried peas, ready for storage

← Snap peas on the vine

SUMMER SQUASH & ZUCCHINI

For the purposes of this book, we'll consider summer squash and zucchini as the same. This also includes scallop squash and any winter squash that's picked when small and used more like a summer squash (more about that in a bit). We eat them all the same way, and their preservation methods are pretty much all the same. When we refer colloquially to "squash" in this section, know that we're referring to any and all types in this family.

Summer squash plants take up a lot of space in the garden, as the plants can grow quite large. Give each plant plenty of room to prevent the crowded conditions that promote fungal diseases like powdery mildew.

PLANNING CONSIDERATIONS: If you have the space and time, plant as many summer squash as possible. The plants are prone to pests (see later section), so hedge your bets. Plant more and you'll outplant the problem. If you think your family needs eight squash plants, plant fifty. By overplanting, you give yourself the wiggle room needed to support heavy losses due to pests while also bringing in a bigger crop all at once, which is great for preservation purposes. We plant fifty to sixty summer squash plants for our family of eight and preserve up to 70 quarts (35 kg) of freeze-dried squash.

SUN REQUIREMENT: Full sun.

GROWING SEASON: Spring and summer; plants are frost sensitive, so wait to plant until the danger of frost has passed.

PESTS: We have to be honest: Summer squash are prone to a lot of pests. Common squash pests

← Give each plant room to grow.

include squash bugs, squash vine borers, and cucumber beetles. If you're a first-time gardener in a new space, chances are good you'll get a year or two before these pests discover your crops. If there was ever a garden nearby, or your neighbors currently have a garden, chances are good that squash bugs will find you by June of your first year. At first they won't be so bad: you can pick the insects and their eggs off of the plants by hand. Eventually, though, you'll notice drooping leaves with yellow speckles, and it will only get worse. This pest pressure can be treated with pesticides, but since we use organic practices in our garden, synthetic chemicals are not an option. Companion planting can help a bit: we plant dill, garlic, onions, and basil near the squash plants to try to confuse these pests. Picking squash bug eggs and cucumber beetles off plants early in the season helps by slowing their annual population growth, but they're sneaky and will quickly outpace your efforts through breeding. We also start our squash plants early in the greenhouse, about two to three weeks before we want to plant them out; this gives the plants a head start toward maturity before the pest pressure gets too great.

↑ Summer squash ready to be preserved

↙ Squash bug eggs

↓ Duct tape is the easiest way we've found to remove squash bug eggs from leaves.

For organic pesticide options, neem oil and diatomaceous earth are effective against squash bug eggs and nymphs. We've mentioned Bt (*Bacillus thuringiensis*) earlier: it can be effective against squash vine borers, but only if applied to the base of the stems weekly and after rain, as it washes off easily.

If you use neem oil, remember that it should only be applied around dusk or right after to avoid harming bees. It has a short half-life and will not be potent by morning, which is good for beneficial insects and pollinators.

HARVESTING: Cut the fruit's stem from the vine when the skin is still soft and the seeds have not yet formed. For most varieties this is when they are less than 8 inches (20 cm) in length.

VARIETIES WE LOVE

When choosing summer squash varieties, you have to consider pest pressure. We love to grow certain heirloom varieties, knowing that we'll lose a good percentage of our harvest.

A freeze-dryer load of sliced squash

When it comes to high production, hybrid varieties are the way to go. Hybrid varieties produce more summer squash faster, and when it comes to pests, they can be more resilient. You really can't go wrong with any summer squash varieties, but these are our favorites.

Hybrid Varieties

- 'Goldmine'
- 'Safari'
- 'Golden Glory'
- 'Noche'
- 'Multipik'
- 'Green Machine'
- 'Spineless Perfection'

Heirloom Varieties

- 'Gray'
- 'Black Beauty'
- 'Early Prolific' straightneck squash
- 'Golden'
- 'Early Golden' crookneck squash
- Zucchino rampicante (also on our winter squash list)

PRESERVATION

Our favorite method of summer squash preservation is freeze-drying. We slice the fruits into approximately ⅓ inch (8 mm) slices and freeze-dry them flat. For storage, we primarily use quart-sized canning jars, while we put some of our produce in Mylar bags for long-term storage.

To use freeze-dried squash in a stir-fry or as fried squash, we rehydrate with cold tap water for about ten minutes, resulting in a slightly floppy slice that can be easily handled during cooking. This is where the quart canning jars come in handy. Simply open them up, remove the oxygen absorber, fill with water, wait, strain, and cook.

You don't need a freeze-dryer to preserve your summer squash, however, as freezing is also an option. Blanch your squash before you freeze it. A very quick blanch (just a few seconds) in water just under a boil, followed by a quick cooldown in ice water, will give you the best texture and flavor. Since squash is prone to freezer burn due to its high moisture content, for best results use vacuum-sealed freezer bags. Puréed or grated squash is great for breads and soups, and they freeze efficiently in either form.

We also preserve zucchini powder for making zucchini bread (though we prefer pumpkin bread if available; the flavor from using pumpkin, even in a zucchini cake recipe, is superior in our opinion). Zucchini powder or shredded zucchini can be dehydrated and used in baking. You can dehydrate your squash and store it as a powder or in shreds for bread. The flavor doesn't stand out, but when baked as an ingredient it can be a great addition.

Some people also use zucchini powder as a kind of flour in baking. While it is really the same thing, powder or flour, the implied uses are a bit different.

If you find you have extra zucchini and summer squash, you can also make sweet or dill relish or pickles with it—simply substitute the cucumbers in your pickle or relish recipe with zucchini or summer squash. Home pressure canning of zucchini and summer squash is not recommended, but you can safely pickle zucchini. The added acid in these types of recipes makes it safe.

In years when we have a bad cucumber crop, we fall back on squash for pickling, and no one can tell the difference. Can traditional squash pickles/relish or make fermented ones, just like the cucumber recipe found in the cucumber produce profile on page 157.

→ Sliced squash ready for use

CUCUMBERS

Cucumber vines can grow quite large. Save space by growing them vertically up a trellis or along a fence.

PLANNING CONSIDERATIONS: Cucumbers produce vines that need to climb, though compact bush varieties are available. In our garden we've always planted vining cucumbers between cherry tomato plants. They have similar soil, sun, and water needs, and cucumbers and tomatoes don't share pests. When we've tried to plant cucumbers in their own space—for example, along the outer garden fence—they've experienced much more and earlier pest pressure than when they're planted between the tomato plants. Cucumbers can be incredibly easy to grow; in our garden, though, they're always a challenge due to pest pressure and our maintaining organic practices.

Think about pest pressure when planning how many cucumbers you will need grow: the effect of pests on your growing strategy can mean all or nothing (see pests section below). Plant two or three cucumber plants per family member for fresh eating, or three to four cucumber plants per quart of pickles you want to preserve. We've never planted that many, but in a good year we can plant ten to fifteen cucumber plants and make all the pickles we could ever want. If it's a bad cucumber beetle year, we may only get one or two cucumbers from the same number of plants. This past year was particularly awful, as we didn't plant our cucumbers with our tomatoes and we had a mild winter, resulting in greater and earlier pest pressure. We lost half of our twenty-five cucumber transplants before they even bloomed; the cause was bacterial wilt, which is a pathogen spread

← Homegrown cucumbers are full of crunch and flavor.

by cucumber beetles. A few varieties of pickling cucumbers held on, but they still had a great deal of trouble producing because cucumber beetles eat the pollen out of flowers (among other things), which interferes with pollination.

Another way to plan cucumber plantings is to consider that, under ideal circumstances (a pest-free garden), you'll likely get 1 to 3 pounds (454 g to 1.4 kg) of cucumbers per plant per week for up to twelve weeks, and you'll need 1 to 2 pounds (454 to 907 g) per quart of pickles. We always pickle our cucumbers in pints because we prefer that size for eating. This means that, with ten plants, you'd have enough cucumbers in less than a week to make a batch (7 or 8 pints [3.3 or 3.8 L]) of pickles. If you don't expect your plants to last long due to pest pressure, raise that number accordingly and you'll probably be alright.

Have too many cucumbers? If you have some farm animals, this is never a problem: Chickens *love* them, as do rabbits, pigs, and goats. You can also add them to your water for a refreshing summer treat.

SUN REQUIREMENT: Full sun.

GROWING SEASON: Spring and summer; cucumbers are not frost tolerant and should not be planted until the danger of frost has passed.

PESTS: We're not trying to scare you out of planting cucumbers, but it's important to note that cucumbers are cucurbits (see squash section)—this means they're in the same family as squash and melons, and they share a lot of the same pest pressure. While squash bugs prefer squash and zucchini, cucumber beetles are aptly named for their preference of cucumbers. Preference just means cucumbers are their first choice, but these pests will attack anything in the cucurbit family. There are multiple types of cucumber beetles—striped and spotted, eastern and western—which can be found throughout most of the United States, Canada, Mexico, and Europe. If you have cucumber beetles but don't plant cucumbers, or if they've already destroyed your cucumbers, these little yellow pests will go after your squash and melons. Spotted cucumber beetles will even attack other plants such as cosmos, dahlias, tomatoes, among others. If you've never seen cucumber beetles in your garden, consider yourself lucky and keep an eye out for them. If you spot them, you can knock them back before they spread disease and destruction all over your garden.

So what can be done about cucumber beetles? Organic methods to control them include spinosad, neem, diatomaceous earth, cucumber beetle traps (with pheromones to attract them), yellow sticky traps, and beneficial nematodes (see sidebar below). Every one of these methods—with the exception of the nematodes—also harms or has the potential to harm beneficial insects. We've tried them all, and none of them has made a major difference in our cucumber beetle infestation. The beneficial nematodes did seem to help, but it took a couple years of consistent application for us to really see results.

HARVESTING: Cut cucumbers from their vines when they reach the desired size. For pickling whole, harvest cucumbers younger and smaller. For spears or slices, they can be a little larger. However, you'll want to harvest before the seeds fully develop and the skin toughens and changes color.

BENEFICIAL NEMATODES

These naturally occurring, microscopic organisms can be found in the soil throughout the world. They parasitize and kill some of the insects we consider pests while in their ground-dwelling larval or pupal stage of development. When you introduce these nematodes into your soil, they locate pests and enter their bodies, producing bacteria that kill the host pest while the nematodes continue to reproduce within it, spreading their population to tackle future pests.

VARIETIES WE LOVE

Our favorite slicing cucumber varieties include 'Marketmore 76', 'Muncher', and the Asian cucumber, 'Noky'.

'Monika' is our favorite dual-purpose cucumber. This cucumber also does not require pollination, which means you can cover it with insect netting in an attempt to keep the cucumber beetles and other pests away without negatively impacting pollination. There are several other self-pollinating cucumber varieties as well: look for them in your favorite seed catalog.

For pickling cucumbers, we've had good luck with 'Chicago Pickling' and 'National Pickling'. The hybrid variety called 'Pick-a-Bushel' has always performed well for us too.

PRESERVATION

We hope we haven't talked you out of growing cucurbits. While the pest pressure and belief in using organic practices make them challenging, when it comes time to preserve cucumbers, all the hard work and heartache is worth it. We hope that the warnings and all of the pest suggestions that have worked for us help you enjoy a bountiful harvest!

Pickling is by far the most popular way to preserve cucumbers. We'll break this down into vinegar-brine picking and fermenting. There are other methods, but they're not ones we use or have found to be very popular.

The kind of pickles people tend to think of are produced through vinegar-brine pickling. These are your traditional restaurant-style dill pickles, sweet pickles, or hot dog relish. They're the most popular because they have an extremely long shelf life, can be mass produced, and they travel well. While they're tasty and are a staple in our house, fermented pickles have become our favorite. We urge you to try this kind of pickle once you begin your preservation journey. They are tasty and have a crunchy texture. Even better, it's so

Dill pickles on our pantry shelves

rewarding to discover a food you didn't previously know about because it isn't mass produced. It can be extra pleasing to know you can make something so satisfying in your own kitchen!

In chapter 4, we dove into the basics and benefits of fermentation, so we won't cover that subject again here. We'll add, however, that there are extra things you can do with fermented pickles that aren't possible—or at least aren't as good—with vinegar-brined pickles. One of these is creating freeze-dried or dehydrated pickle chips. They're a crunchy, healthy treat that doesn't overpower the senses like vinegar-brined pickle chips (trust us, we've tried both). As an added bonus, throw these chips in a blender and make a powder. Try the powder on popcorn or chicken, or mix it with sour cream to make a zesty dip!

Frozen cucumbers can be used in dips, smoothies, baked goods, and soups where the mushy texture isn't an issue. Plain freeze-dried cucumbers can be rehydrated and used in these types of recipes as well. Tzatziki sauce is another great way to use frozen cucumbers.

Like other cucurbits, you can use cucumbers as a baking ingredient. Cucumber cake, which uses frozen or powdered cucumber, is an old recipe that's popular, but try it before you grow cucumbers for it, because the flavor is powerful and it's not for everyone.

You can even make cucumbers into a jam or jelly. Cucumber mint jam and cucumber melon jelly are popular variations. We know it sounds weird and, yes, there are some strange jams and jellies mentioned in this book, but they're all pretty great. When in doubt, the internet is another resource for finding recipes and ideas. Chances are good that someone somewhere has tried making everything into a jam or jelly. It's one of the safest ways to preserve foods, because the sugar or added acid creates an environment where botulism cannot grow.

FERMENTED OLD-FASHIONED DILL PICKLES

INGREDIENTS

6 to 8 small pickling cucumbers (about 3 inches [7.5 cm] long) or 2 large pickling cucumbers quartered
4 cups (948 ml) water
2 tablespoons (36 g) salt
2 to 4 cloves garlic
1 head dill plant
2 4-inch (10 cm) sprigs of dill
1 grape leaf (optional, but helps preserve crispness)
1 teaspoon black peppercorns (optional)
1 teaspoon yellow mustard seeds (optional)

INSTRUCTIONS

Soak the cucumbers in a bath of ice water for at least 30 minutes; this helps keep them crisp.

Dry cucumbers, then cut off the ends. Slice or quarter the cucumbers. Pack them into the jar(s).

Add the spices, dill and grape leaf (if desired)

Mix the salt and water together, stir until salt is dissolved. Pour the salt brine over the cucumbers.

The cucumbers need to be submerged at least 1 inch (2.5 cm) below the surface of the brine. We use a fermentation weight for this. A fermentation lid is helpful as well, but you can use a cloth or burp the pickles once a day.

Leave in a dark place for up to one week (not the fridge). Taste after two to three days; the cooler your house the longer they will take to ferment.

Transfer to the fridge or cold storage like a root cellar—shelf life in cool storage is six to nine months.

CELERY

Celery doesn't take up much room in the garden as it tends to grow vertically rather than horizontally. Celery prefers the cooler weather of the spring and is generally ready to harvest in about four months. It prefers full sun with afternoon shade. Celery also needs loose soil; its roots aren't strong enough to deal with crowding, and it doesn't favor rocky or otherwise compacted soil.

We aren't going to pretend to be experts when it comes to growing celery. We've never grown a bunch of celery comparable to what you buy in the grocery store. This is because celery needs to be blanched—which has nothing to do with boiling water, but simply means shielding the plant from light—to grow tall and look and taste like the celery you recognize. Most people blanch their celery in order to prevent it from tasting bitter, but my unblanched celery has never been bitter. It's been tougher, and the flavor is much stronger than any store-bought celery we've tasted before. For us, this works because we use celery in recipes for the flavor, not the texture.

PLANNING CONSIDERATIONS: If you want to try blanching your celery, wrap newspaper, brown paper, or paper bags around the plants and tie it with something that can stretch; pantyhose work well for this. You can also use milk cartons to surround the plant, bury the plant in a trench, or place boards on either side of the row—anything to block the light and help the plant grow taller. When blanching, remember to cover the stalks only and not the leaves. Blanching needs to be done two to three weeks before harvest. You can also try a self-blanching celery variety.

← We typically dedicate half of a raised bed to celery.

SUN REQUIREMENT: Full sun with afternoon shade.

GROWING SEASON: Spring and summer.

PESTS: Grasshoppers can be a significant pest for celery, as they feed on the tender leaves and stems. They typically chew large holes in the foliage, leading to a ragged appearance and weakening the plant. Their feeding can stunt the growth of celery and reduce the overall yield. Grasshoppers tend to cause the most damage in warm, dry conditions; if not controlled, they can quickly defoliate a celery plant, making it more susceptible to diseases.

HARVESTING: Slice the plant off at its base, just above where it meets the soil. Harvesting is best done when the plant reaches the days-to-maturity noted on the seed packet.

VARIETIES WE LOVE

We recommend self-blanching varieties such as 'Golden Self-Blanching' or 'Utah Tall' celery. We've grown 'Utah Tall'—while the flavor was great, the stalks were very narrow. Like everything with gardening, we'll keep trying, and you should too! There's no reason to waste "failed" celery crops—see below for information on how we've preserved our celery even when it didn't look like what you'd get at the store.

PRESERVATION

Our homegrown celery tastes much stronger than the store-bought equivalent, probably the result of not blanching the stems properly, in our case. With produce that has a stronger taste, less is more in most recipes. Celery leaves can be dehydrated, frozen, or freeze-dried. The stalks can also be preserved by any of these methods, diced for soups, stews, and casseroles. Since our kids don't like the texture of celery, we prefer to make a dehydrated or freeze-dried celery powder to add flavor without the texture. You can also make a celery salt using the celery leaves and salt to dry out and absorb the flavor of the celery. If you've used celery salt from the grocery store, chances are good it was made with celery seeds, so the flavor will be a bit different.

Celery seeds can also be used and preserved. Celery is a biennial plant that blooms in its second year. For this to happen, it needs to survive the winter to be able to produce seed.

Celery has natural nitrates and can be juiced, dehydrated, and then used as a powder to cure meats at home. Be sure to consult a reliable recipe concerning the appropriate amount of celery powder to use in curing meats.

Celery can also be stored in a root cellar. Like other root cellar veggies, it prefers a temperature just above freezing, 32°F to 40°F (0°C to 4.4°C), and high humidity for optimum storage.

ONIONS

We love onions. We grow a *lot* of onions. From yellow sweet onions and white onions to 'Red Candy Apple' onions, we grow more onions than most normal families our size. This is partly because we love them in all sorts of dishes and it's a rare meal we prepare that doesn't have onions in it. This also has to do with the fact that they cellar very well, and we can have fresh onions for a good portion of the calendar year. They're also versatile in preservation methods.

PLANNING CONSIDERATIONS: There are three main ways to start and grow onions: from seed, from sets, and from starts. There are pros and cons to each method.

STARTING ONIONS FROM SEEDS

Use fresh seeds if you choose this method, as older seeds likely won't germinate (even year-old seeds can germinate dramatically less well than other plant seeds). Direct-seeding onions doesn't work in cooler climates, so you'd have to live somewhere with a very mild climate for this to be viable. Seeds need to be started indoors under grow lights for three to four months before planting them out. Thankfully they don't take up much space: Onions seeds can be spread on a small tray. They grow like grass when they're small.

As they grow, cut the tops off and give them a "haircut" to let them get thicker. Once planting time comes around and the roots are about ½ inch (1 cm) across (they can be smaller and still work out), plant them as you would plant any starts.

← Freshly harvested onions, ready to cure or preserve

When you grow from seed, you're basically growing your own onion starts.

Pros: This method saves you money and allows you access to varieties you may not be able to purchase as starts.

Cons: You'll spend four months growing something in potentially inhospitable weather that would cost a few dollars if you bought it in a store. Depending on how many onions you're growing, starting from seed may not make sense. Locally, for us, a bundle of fifty onion starts (retail at a local nursery) costs about two times what a packet of onion seeds would. To us, it's worth buying starts and saving the space and time that would otherwise have been spent nurturing the seeds for three or four months.

STARTING ONIONS FROM STARTS

Once you have your onion starts—either having purchased or grown them—plant them out about six weeks before your last frost date. Onions can handle freezing temperatures if they're planted properly. For most years, our onions experience temperatures in the low teens and single digits and still thrive. Before an intense freeze, it can help to make sure your soil is not too dry, and if you are going to experience a late freeze after it's been really warm, cover them with frost cloth or a sheet to protect the new tender green tops from damage.

Pros: Inexpensive, and there's no need to handle delicate seedlings or grow them indoors under grow lights.

Cons: Sometimes onion starts purchased from the store will bloom, depending on how long they're out of the ground (because they will be pulled, bundled, and kept dry during transport to prevent mold). This is why, when planting starts, it's extremely important to get fresh ones.

STARTING ONIONS FROM SETS

Onions are a biennial plant: In year one they grow, in year two they bloom. Onion sets are small bulbs grown the previous year, essentially tricked into thinking it's their second year because they've gone dormant and then come back. Onions that bloom taste different, don't store as well, and often have a woody center.

Pros: Starts are widely available and easy to plant.

Cons: Sets may flower instead of producing big bulbs.

ONION SPACING TIPS

We've experimented with a lot of different spacing for onions. We rarely get big onion bulbs in our climate, so we don't exclusively plant them 4 inches (10 cm) apart as recommended. We plant most of our starts 2 inches (5 cm) apart, in a zigzag pattern if in a row or, if planting in a bed, we plant them 4 to 6 inches (10 to 15 cm) apart using weed fabric (where the weed/grass pressure is high) with burned planting holes, planting two or three onion starts in each hole. Using this method, if the soil is soft enough, we end up with two or three medium onions versus a single large one. With the zigzag row, we can harvest smaller onions early and let the larger ones continue growing. This gives us the opportunity to eat onions straight from the garden in May and June, harvesting the rest in late June and early July (four months after planting).

PLANTING DEPTH MATTERS

Planting depth is important with onions. Only plant about ½ inch (1 cm) of the start or half of the bulb underground. If you plant them too deep, they won't make a bulb. This doesn't seem deep enough, but trust us—it's what you want. The roots are on the very bottom, so that's what you want in the dirt, not the whole baby bulb.

An early harvest of green beans and onions—destined to be eaten fresh

In mid-summer, we devote our outdoor kitchen area to curing onions and garlic.

↑ Canned French onion soup base

→ Onions after curing, ready to be taken down

SUN REQUIREMENT: Full sun.

GROWING SEASON: Plant in very early spring and harvest later in the summer.

PESTS: Onions are the best plants when it comes to pests—because there really aren't any! In fact, onions repel more pests than they fall victim to. We do have an onion patch in our garden, but we interplant onions with other crops to deter early spring pests like aphids.

HARVESTING: Harvest onions when 50 percent of your plants of any given variety have yellowed and fallen over. It will look like a windstorm came through and pushed a bunch of your onions over. Some people will tell you to knock over the rest of the onions, but that isn't necessary. Just harvest them within a week or two of them falling over, quicker if the weather is very wet.

As we mentioned earlier, one reason we love onions so much is that, with proper planning and work, they store well. The two key points to getting long storage out of your onions are variety selection and proper curing.

As a general rule, the sweeter the onion, the less shelf life it will have. We grow different varieties with different levels of sweetness and use them accordingly. If properly stored, they will begin to sprout before rotting, so you aren't under the gun as much as with other vegetables. Once we notice a lot of sprouting in our cellar, we make a determination based on how many we have left as to whether we need to keep using them as we have or to do some impromptu preservation (see below). As a general rule, we still get five to seven months of storage out of our sweetest onions, and would probably get more if we had better climate control for them.

To keep onions in your cellar, it's important to cure them properly. We cure our onions in our outdoor kitchen: it's a warm, covered outdoor space with good airflow but protection from the sun. This is the best setting for curing onions.

To cure them, we hang them from a mesh screen by their tops and leave them (sometimes with a fan blowing on them) until the tops are completely dry and crunchy. This process can take weeks. Once you're sure they're completely dried out, cut off the tops a few inches above the bulb (again, make sure it's dry all the way through). Onions can be stored long-term in the fridge, but this environment is really a bit too cold and dry. A root cellar is best, with temperatures around 40°F (4°C) and a humidity level between 60 and 70 percent.

As mentioned, we grow all different types of onions. With proper curing, the sweetest ones last five to seven months, and the more savory, less-sweet ones can last through the winter.

VARIETIES WE LOVE

Some varieties that are known to store well include:

- 'Copra'
- 'Sweet Sandwich'
- 'Red Zeppelin'

Varieties that are mid-range for storage and still among our favorites for flavor are:

- 'Walla Walla'
- 'Candy'

Unfortunately our very favorite onions, the 'Red Candy Apple' onion and 'Super Star', are not considered good for storing, but they still last in our home at room temperature for five to seven months.

Two different types of dehydrated onions in the pantry

PRO TIP

If you plan on dehydrating a lot of onions and peppers every year, consider a dehydrator that has stainless-steel parts that can be deep cleaned, or alternately a dedicated, cheaper dehydrator just for onions and peppers.

Depending on your goals, any onion may be just fine for storage. Most years, we're still eating onions that aren't known to be good for storage well into December. We generally grow a combination of all of these and use or preserve them based on how they age.

PRESERVATION

How you preserve your onions will depend a lot on how you use onions. There are several options.

Dehydrated onions are a great option. They're best diced very small, which allows them to rehydrate more quickly. Many recipes call for dehydrated diced onions. You can also put your dehydrated onions in a high-powered blender and make onion powder. The downside of dehydrating onions is that, if your dehydrator has plastic trays or parts, the strong odor of the onions can permeate the plastic and cause the smell to linger forever. Running a dehydrator full of onions (or

A jar of our freeze-dried onions

spicy peppers) indoors can also be quite unpleasant. We frequently run our dehydrator on our covered screen porch outside—if it's particularly humid or rainy, the process can take longer, but on a typical summer or early fall day it's comparable to running the unit indoors.

One great option for preserving onions is making onion salt. Similar to dehydrated onion, onion salt involves dicing or blending onions and then mixing them with salt, similar to the herb salts discussed earlier in this book. This allows the salt to absorb the flavor of the onions while drying the onions, and you get a tasty salt. Drying onion salts will take a lot longer than the herb salts due to the higher moisture content of onions versus most herbs, but it's well worth it. We love making onion salt with 'Red Candy Apple' onions, as it results in a beautiful pink salt that tastes like caramelized onions when added to steamed or stir-fried veggies.

Freeze-drying is another great method for preserving onions. Slivered, freeze-dried onions are so versatile: They can be crushed into a powder, stirred into soups, stews, or casseroles without any further prep, or they can be rehydrated and used as you would use frozen-thawed onions. They have a shelf life of up to thirty years when stored properly. The flavor of freeze-dried onions is comparable to fresh onions. Unlike dehydrating, freeze-drying onions doesn't affect the flavor of other foods inside the freeze-dryer. As long as the foods aren't touching, you can freeze-dry onions with other vegetables without a change in flavor.

Freeze-drying onions does result in a strong onion smell, either during the process or after, when the freeze-dryer is defrosting. If your freeze-dryer is in your house, plan on processing them on a day when you can have the windows open.

It's worth noting that freeze-dried onions are very delicate. They have the consistency of Styrofoam, and they store best in canning jars for their protection. While you can store them in Mylar bags, without a lot of special care, expect a lot of them to end up as onion powder.

Still another way to preserve onions is by freezing them. Dice onions, freeze them on a baking sheet and then, once frozen, place them in zipper-top plastic bags or vacuum bags. Vacuum-sealed onions will last longer but, depending on how long you need them to last, just pressing the air out of a zipper-top bag will do. It's handy to reach in the freezer and grab a handful of diced onion out of a gallon bag and go about your day.

If you're looking to can onions, a couple of options are pickled onions (which can be water-bathed) or French onion soup (which is pressure canned). Onions can also be used as a flavor-enhancing ingredient in other canning recipes such as salsa, green beans, soups, chili, and more.

A downside to processing onions is that it can be a miserable experience. Using a mandolin slicer, food processor, or other chopping gadget to speed up the process is invaluable. We like to have a turning fan blowing in the kitchen to circulate the air or, if it's not too hot outside, chopping onions in the open air can help avoid suffering with burning eyes and tears.

GROWING AND PRESERVING GREEN ONIONS

Green onions are the tender, green tops of your onions. They add a mild onion flavor and beautiful color to any savory dish, they can be used in place of chives in recipes. They can also be frozen, freeze-dried, or even dehydrated for preservation. Green onions can be grown from specialty varieties that grow more greens, grow longer, and don't produce a large bulb, or you can just use the more tender parts of the green tops off your regular onions. We dice them up and both freeze-dry and dehydrate some every year.

CORN

We have less experience growing corn than many other crops because it's only been recently that we've had the space to experiment with this crop. You don't need lot of space to grow corn, but in a small space corn comes with its own rules and challenges.

PLANNING CONSIDERATIONS: There are three main types of corn grown in the home garden: sweet corn, field corn (also known as dent corn, for corn meal or corn flour), and popping corn.

Corn needs wind to pollinate, so multiple corn plants must be planted together in a block rather than in a single row. Grow at least a 6 x 6-foot (1.8 x 1.8 m) area of corn for the best pollination. Unlike other plants, cross-pollination can change your corn. Growing popcorn with sweet corn, for example, can make your sweet corn less sweet and can even change your popcorn's ability to pop. Because of this, we grow one type of corn per year. If you can separate your corn patches by at least 400 yards (366 m), you may be able to prevent cross-pollination and grow more than one variety per season.

One way to get more out of your corn is to grow popcorn and use it for corn meal. Popcorn and dent corn are dried on the plant and can be stored in an airtight container—no preservation needed! If you're looking to grow corn for cornmeal, we recommend growing popcorn. That way you have a dual-purpose crop, since popcorn also makes great cornmeal.

Corn needs warm soil to germinate, around 60°F (16°C). While it's not recommended to trans-

← Corn plants can be planted fairly close together and need multiple plants in order to pollinate.

plant corn seedlings, it can be done. This past year we couldn't get our corn planted because of excessive rain, so we started half of it in a 128-cell plug tray. Soon after it sprouted, we transplanted it and it took off and grew as well as the direct-sown corn. The key is to transplant your corn when it's quite small—you don't want to let it really establish a root system in a pot.

Plant at least twenty plants in a succession to have enough pollen in the air for the corn to properly pollinate. Our favorite corn varieties to grow in a smaller space are 'Mini Pink' and 'Mini Blue' popcorn; this type of corn makes two to three small ears per plant. Corn is a grass—like your lawn, it has shallow roots and needs to be watered consistently to perform its best, so consider planting your corn in a space where you have easy access to watering or irrigation. The general recommendation is 1 inch (2.5 cm) of water per week. In our experience, popcorn and dent corn don't need quite that much, but they won't complain about it either. Sweet corn on the other hand needs to be kept moist, especially during pollination and ear development. It needs more consistent watering than other types of corn.

Growing field corn or dent corn is an easy way to grow some of your own grain. You can use it to make cornmeal or to feed your animals.

If you want to grow corn for fresh eating, canning, freezing, or freeze-drying, select sweet corn. We've never had great luck with sweet corn, despite being out in the garden daily—we just have trouble keeping a close eye on sweet corn to be sure to harvest it at the right time.

We typically purchase our sweet corn from a small local farm. We could probably grow it ourselves, but most years we'd rather use our space for a variety that doesn't require so much babysitting. Popcorn or dent corn crops offer more of a "plant it and forget it situation," and you're more likely to get a decent crop from these.

SUN REQUIREMENT: Full sun.

GROWING SEASON: Late spring and summer; corn is not tolerant of frost.

PESTS: There's a high risk your sweet corn will be stolen when it's almost ready—raccoons or other garden visitors are the usual culprits. There are several pests that attack corn: some are sneaky, like the spotted cucumber beetle in its larva stage, or the corn earworms that, as their name suggests, feed on the ears themselves. Almost every time you buy fresh corn from a local farmer, whether sprayed with pesticides or not, you'll find a few corn earworms. They're typically just at the tip of the ear and don't destroy the whole thing. Carefully timed application of Bt (see above) can stop corn earworms when sprayed on the silks once they've formed; be sure to reapply after it rains. Bt is considered safe for humans and is approved for organic gardening; plus, in this case, it isn't going directly on the part of the corn you'll eat.

HARVESTING: Harvest corn by snapping the ears off the stalks. Popcorn and dent corn should be harvested only after the stalks have browned and the kernels are fully dry. Sweet corn should be harvested when the kernels are plump, firm, and milky, and the silks have turned brown.

VARIETIES WE LOVE

As we mentioned earlier, we don't grow our own sweet corn. When we buy it, we look for bicolored corn like the 'Peaches and Cream' variety. For popcorn, we generally try a couple new types every year, but our go-tos are the 'Strawberry', 'Mini Pink', and 'Mini Blue' varieties. We find that miniature popcorn varieties fit better in a smaller garden space and can be planted closer together.

PRESERVATION

We love to preserve sweet corn. Our favorite preservation method is freeze-drying, followed by pressure canning, freezing, and dehydrating. We prefer freeze-drying because it's shelf stable, tasty, easy to prepare, and doesn't require blanching.

Let's discuss pressure canning first. Many people recommend blanching corn before canning, but we skip that step as it seems entirely unnecessary when you're already going to be pressure canning at a high temperature.

There are several ways to measure how much you'll need for canning. To fill a 1-quart (946 ml) jar, you'll need about 4½ pounds (2 kg) of corn (in the husk), or 2¼ pounds per pint jar (1 kg per 473 ml). The average ear of corn has just under 1 cup (158 g) of kernels. If you're purchasing corn from a farmers' market or local farm, it's likely sold by the dozen ears. If you want to have enough for one canner-load of pints, you'll need about two dozen ears of sweet corn. Don't forget to purchase a few extras to enjoy fresh corn on the cob.

Freezing corn is nice because you can freeze it on or off the cob. Then there's the question of blanching: honestly, we've blanched sweet corn before freezing and we've decided to skip it. The thinking is, if you don't blanch it, active enzymes will remain in your corn, even while frozen, that will degrade the flavor and nutritional value of the corn. If you're freezing it in summer and plan to eat it over the winter, this probably doesn't matter. At least, that's what we've told ourselves when we didn't blanch it, and we've never noted any

↑ Shucked corn being processed

→ Freeze-dried corn

difference. So, to blanch or not to blanch—it's up to you. If you plan to eat it on the cob and have a lot of freezer space, this method can be great. You can husk your corn or freeze it on the cob right in the husk—what better way to keep your corn from getting freezer burn than by using nature's packaging? We typically cut off the end of the cob for a more uniform size and shape, because there's no reason to keep the silks. If you plan to eat your corn on the cob, this makes the most sense, but if not you're taking up a lot of space and pushing off the work of cutting it off the cob for another day.

If you prefer to eat it off the cob, you should remove it before freezing. Again, to blanch or not to blanch—it's your call. Once the corn is cut off the cob, we prefer using vacuum-sealed freezer bags.

For a small two-serving side dish, add 1½ to 2 cups (237 to 316 g) of corn to the bag and (optionally) include 1 tablespoon (14 g) of butter to each bag; increase the amount you put in each

bag to match the serving size you need. Then, instead of thawing, you can microwave the bag (cut a slit for steam to escape) to prepare the corn. This way of freezing corn allows you to have small, mostly flat bags that are easier to stack in the freezer than the complete corn on the cob.

Freeze-drying corn off the cob is another way we preserve our sweet corn harvest. This past summer we purchased twenty dozen ears of sweet corn from a local farm and freeze-dried about 60 total pints (19 kg). This came out to be a bit less than we should have had based on the measurements for canning so many ears, but this may be because either the kernels shrank slightly from freeze-drying, or the ears were slightly smaller than we'd calculated. Or perhaps because we ate a lot of it fresh.

All in all, freezing or freeze-drying corn will give you the closest flavor to fresh sweet corn.

Fermenting is a more unusual way to preserve sweet corn. Sour corn is a popular side dish in the South, made from lacto-fermenting sweet corn using a method similar to making sauerkraut, though it doesn't significantly increase the shelf life and the product is not shelf stable.

TREE FRUITS

Pears, Peaches, Cherries, Plums, Persimmons

If you want to grow your own orchard, remember that it will be at least five years before you get much usable fruit, but it will be worth the wait.

Growing the right fruit trees for your area and knowing if it's worth planting any at all will be key to your planning. We chose what to plant in our orchard based on a few factors. The first was our space: we had a lot to work with. Then, to choose the trees, we purchased those that other locals were growing successfully and also ones that were available on clearance from local nurseries. If you have the space, trees on clearance that are available locally aren't the worst choice, even without any prior research. You never know what will do well. We don't, however, recommend buying random trees online that you know nothing about. Honestly, we don't like to order trees online at all, preferring instead to be able to see the tree, the graft union, and also, when buying local, choosing larger trees than what can be purchased online and shipped.

Our orchard is eight years old now, and we've learned a lot since we began it. While there isn't much we'd do differently, we haven't had great luck with it. What had the biggest impact on our orchard was about our microclimate: had we waited a few years, we probably would not have tried to grow an orchard at all. That's a risk we don't regret taking, and we're still adding fruit trees despite what we've learned.

One year, the weather will be perfect and we'll have the harvest of a lifetime. As discussed in the section on what to grow versus what to buy (page 34), in our area temperatures tend to be warm enough to get the fruit trees to bloom, then we get a late freeze that limits their production. Sometimes we lose 50 percent of our harvest, sometimes we lose 100 percent. But with our microclimate—we tend to get about 8°F (-13°C) colder than our neighbors—frost settles faster along our property that runs alongside a creek, and that makes all the difference when it comes to fruit trees. So some years, we lose 75 percent of our fruit while our neighbors less than a mile away have a nice harvest, and other years our entire area loses all of the peaches, pears, or cherries to late frost.

Hopefully all this isn't too discouraging, as fruit trees are usually worth the risk because the reward, when it does work out, is so great. Just two years ago we planted a few more sour cherry trees right by our house: we figured, if we get no usable fruit from them, at least they'll bloom and be beautiful. This year they bloomed and made tons of little cherries, but we lost 90 percent of the fruit in a late freeze.

↑ A peach ripening in our orchard

← Harvested peaches about to be skinned, sliced, and canned

PLANNING CONSIDERATIONS: Fruit trees need to be pruned annually in the winter. There are two primary methods of pruning based on the type of trees you have. Pruning techniques are beyond the scope of this book, but know it's something you'll need to research based on your trees.

Another nice thing about having an orchard is that, when you trim branches, you can use them to smoke meat (applewood smoked bacon anyone?). If you raise rabbits, they love to chew on fruit sticks.

If you're worried about varieties or the care the trees need, grow fruits that are native to your area. In our part of the country, we can grow persimmons, mulberries, wild plums, and pawpaws. These local trees don't tend to have the issues that more popular fruit trees have.

Mulberries and persimmons require a male and female tree to fruit. These trees grow like weeds on our farm, they look nice and are fast-growing trees, but they don't produce decorative flowers. We love them because their fruits are tasty when made into pies, jams, jelly, and wine, and they also attract birds that eat them instead of going straight for our blackberries.

Wild plums produce beautiful blooms, they're small and not great to eat fresh, but they make amazing jelly and wine.

Fruit trees can be grown in a relatively small space for landscaping, in a traditional orchard, or as part of a food forest or permaculture space. We can't list all the possibilities here!

In addition, fruit trees could be grown to the west of your garden to provide afternoon shade for your heat-sensitive garden plants. There are many dwarf varieties available for smaller spaces. Always check the varieties you plant to see if they need two trees to pollinate each other or if they're self-pollinating.

HARVESTING: Each tree fruit has a different harvest window and different signs of harvest readiness. Read up on each variety you grow to ensure a well-timed harvest.

VARIETIES WE LOVE

Peaches

The 'Reliance' peach is a cold hardy variety, giving it a chance to produce in cooler climates. The blossoms tend to be more hardy to frost and are generally are later blooming than other varieties.

Pears

'Kieffer' pear is a hybrid between European and Asian pears, great for canning and preserving.

Asian pears, such as 'Shinko' are delicious. They are round—shaped more like an apple—so not the traditional pear shape.

Sour Cherries

'Montmorency' cherries are very tart and make amazing cherry pie filling or cherry preserves. They are also rich in antioxidants.

Mulberries

Mulberries grow wild in our area, though there are lots of cultivated varieties. The wild mulberries we grow are red mulberries and white mulberries. Because we have so many and they are fast growing, we haven't needed to plant any more. However, if we did, we would look for the 'Downing' mulberry or 'Tice' mulberry, both of which are great for canning and preserving. Another benefit to these two domesticated cultivars of mulberry is that they are self-pollinating and do not require a male and female tree like the wild varieties do.

Persimmons

American and Asian persimmons are two different fruits. We've been talking about American persimmons. If you're looking for a cultivated variety of American persimmons, we recommend 'Meader' persimmon and 'Prok' persimmon—both are self-pollinating, so they do not require a male and female tree.

PRESERVATION

When it comes to preserving homegrown tree fruit, we typically make jams and jellies. It's more difficult to get uniform chunks from our organically grown fruit because of imperfections due to insects and hail. The situation is easier when you have fruit that's shaped nicely, as we found in our 50-pound (23-kg) pear harvest last year. Pears ripen off the tree, so even though we harvested them all at once, they didn't all ripen at the same time. As they ripened we peeled and froze them, then were able to make pear preserves from the frozen pears.

We tend to buy most of our tree fruits in bulk to keep our pantry stocked and to meet our goals. Whether we buy or grow the fruit ourselves, the same preservation methods apply.

Freezing is option number one. Nearly all fruits can be frozen. Generally, slice them and freeze on a

↑ Preparing peaches for canning

→ Processed peaches ready for the pantry shelf

tray, then transfer the frozen pieces to a vacuum-sealable bag for long-term storage. These can be great for pies or fresh eating later in the year.

Most fruits can also be freeze-dried, but be aware that cutting uniform pieces of your fruit is important to ensure that your full batch dries. If you have thick slices on a tray with thinner ones, you're more likely to have moisture left in the large pieces, leading to spoilage or at least a decrease in the quality of the stored batch. We love to have freeze-dried apple, peach, and pear slices on the shelf for quick, healthy snacks.

Having six children in the house, we go through a lot of jams and jellies. This method is our go-to for preserving fruits. We use these home-canned goodies in the traditional ways (on toast or PB&J), but we also enjoy them as an alternative to maple syrup on pancakes and waffles.

Canning fruit pieces is another way to preserve them, but it's not something we do for direct consumption. We do can pie filling, though: it's nice to have a 1-quart (946 ml) jar of apple, pear, strawberry, or peach pie filling on the shelf for quick access. There's no worry about having to thaw fruit from the freezer: Just dump it in a pie crust and bake! Also, a jar of apple pie filling topped with a crumb topping and baked makes a super-quick and tasty apple crisp for dessert.

BERRIES

Growing your own berries probably sounds complicated, but there's likely a berry out there that you can easily grow in your space and climate. Growing berries may not seem worth it at first, with the time and money investment involved, but you'll change your mind when you consider how much fresh organic berries cost at the grocery store.

Most berries have similar growing needs. Consistent water and protection from cold when they're blooming and fruiting (this varies based on the plant) are the main considerations. While individual strawberry plants take up much less space than blackberries, raspberries, or blueberries, you need more strawberry plants to grow enough to preserve and eat fresh.

PLANNING CONSIDERATIONS

For our family of eight, our blackberry patch gives us enough blackberries for preserving and fresh eating; it takes up less space than our strawberry patch. We have three 30-foot (9.1 m) rows of trellised thornless blackberries, and around 400 strawberry plants, which take up a lot more space than the trellised blackberries. We have our strawberries planted a bit creatively and too

The strawberry section of our garden

A handful of ripe strawberries

Flowering strawberries

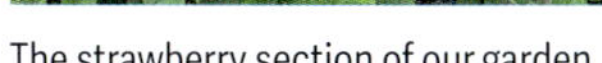

← There's nothing more satisfying than a bowl of ripe blackberries.

close together, which makes harvesting difficult. The recommended spacing is 12 inches (30 cm) between plants, plus a reasonable amount of space to walk between the rows. We planted ours more like we plant our cut flowers, in 3-foot (91 cm) wide rows with 9 inches (23 cm) of spacing. This allowed us to fit many more berries in a smaller space, and they produced great results, but they were quite difficult to harvest and gather all the berries between the plants.

Berries ripen throughout the season, generally in the following order (though there are early and late varieties that can cause overlap, and raspberries and blackberries vary a lot, with some ripening in June and some in August).

- Strawberries
- Blueberries
- Raspberries
- Blackberries

Next, let's take a look at planning considerations for each berry type.

STRAWBERRIES

Plan on around fifty plants per person per year for canning and fresh eating. Strawberries require the most replanting of any of the berries—for maximum efficiency they need to be replanted every year, but for a home gardener, every three to four years may be enough. If you stay on top of taking care of them—rooting runners and replacing plants that are no longer producing with your own stock—then you may be able to keep them much longer.

Strawberry Pests

Birds, rabbits, ants, aphids, tarnished plant bugs, and others. For birds, we have our kids find strawberry-shaped rocks on the farm, paint them red with black dots to resemble mature strawberries,

JUNE-BEARING VERSUS EVERBEARING

June-bearing strawberries don't necessarily ripen in June—here, they tend to bloom in May, but they do make the majority of their berries all at once. This can be much better if you're looking to can strawberry products, or if you don't like to pick berries daily for months on end. We've never been fans of everbearing strawberries because they don't produce enough at once for our large family to really enjoy them, let alone can them. Plus, after three to four weeks of harvesting strawberries, we're over it and don't want to mess with them anymore—likely just when the next type of berry is starting to ripen.

and scatter them in and around the strawberry patch. The birds learn quickly that they aren't yummy and to find better food elsewhere. Netting is also effective for birds, but this can only be used after the flowers have been pollinated.

Excessive rain or sitting on wet ground will quickly make your berries rot, so make sure you're picking frequently if it's wet outside.

Varieties

There are different varieties of strawberries, generally classified as early, mid-, and late-season. What to plant for your area and what works best for you will depend specifically on your climate and, more specifically, your last freeze date.

Preserving

Make strawberry jam, freeze the berries whole, or freeze-dry them in slices. Dehydrated fruit leather is another great way to enjoy your strawberry harvest, though the color will be dark, not bright strawberry red.

BLUEBERRIES

Blueberries thrive in acidic, well-drained soil with a pH between 4.5 and 5.5. They prefer soil that's rich in organic matter and slightly sandy or loamy in texture. Good drainage is essential to prevent waterlogging, which can damage the roots. Adding peat moss or compost can help maintain the acidic conditions and improve soil structure. While this has kept us from growing blueberries in our area, they can be easy to grow in other areas. Plus, no trellis is needed, and while they still must be pruned to remove old growth, at least there are no thorns and the plants are a manageable size.

Flowering blackberries

Varieties

There are dozens of different varieties of blueberries available for planting. Choose the best ones for your climate. You'll need two or more different varieties to get a good fruit set, since the plants require cross-pollination.

Preservation

For canning and preserving, you'll need to grow ten to twenty blueberry plants per person. A mature blueberry plant produces 5 to 10 pounds (2.3 to 4.5 kg) of blueberries per year. You need about 1 to 1½ pounds (454 to 680 g) of blueberries per pint jar (473 ml) of preserves. Blueberries can be frozen or dehydrated.

To freeze-dry blueberries, you need to poke a hole in each berry or they won't dry evenly due to their thick skin. This can be a downside to freeze-drying, as it's quite tedious, but remember that freeze-dried blueberries are very good crunchy, will last for over twenty-five years when stored properly, and can be used in a variety of recipes.

BLACKBERRIES

If you want to grow blackberries, thornless varieties are the way to go. We also highly encourage using a trellis, fence, or wire to keep them in line. We clean up our blackberries once a year, cutting back all the old growth and using twine to tie the new growth to the trellis. If you don't do this, the first year or two would probably be fine, but after that, your blackberries will get out of hand and you won't be able to reach all the berries or get to the base of the plants to fertilize or mulch.

With blackberries, the common thinking is that you need four to six plants per person for enough to preserve. While we started with thirty plants, we're not sure how many we have now because they spread prolifically. We also rooted and transplanted more to fill in our rows. If you've ever grown blackberries, you know it can be difficult to count the actual plants, even if you do have them growing in a relatively neat row.

Varieties

We don't know what variety the majority of our thornless blackberries are because another gardener gave them to us. (As a side note, this is a great way to get started with blackberries, since you know they'll do well in your climate if someone else has so many they need to get rid of them!) Thornless blackberries come in several varieties that ripen at different times throughout the growing season. Varieties that ripen early, like 'Prime-Ark® 45', begin producing fruit in late spring to early summer. In our area, we'd be nervous to try an early blackberry for fear that we would lose the crop to a late frost, but if you live in a milder climate, this might be a good choice for you. Mid-season varieties such as 'Navaho' offer a good balance between yield and fruit quality, ripening in mid-summer. Later-ripening varieties like 'Apache' and 'Triple Crown' produce fruit in late summer to early fall, with some even continuing into autumn. These varieties, known for their large, sweet berries, are especially popular for home gardeners who want a longer harvesting window. Remember, if your primary goal is to preserve berries, you may not want a large harvest window. However, with blackberries, it's easy to freeze them as their ripening progresses and then preserve them later by making fruit leather, preserves, jelly, or even freeze-drying them. They're also good in smoothies and blackberry ice cream.

Preservation

We love to eat blackberries while they're fresh. We freeze the rest just after we pick them. For the producing season, out of our little patch, we will pick 1 to 3 gallons (2.3 to 6.9 kg) a day. We just put them directly in a zipper-top plastic bag and throw them in the deep freeze. Most of these blackberries end up fueling a marathon jelly-making session in the winter, but some also get freeze-dried or made into fruit leather. By far, blackberry jelly is a favorite in our house.

Fresh red raspberries from our patch

RASPBERRIES

Raspberries are another perennial berry that typically grow as thorny, woody shrubs. Even thornless raspberries have thorns. Their growth habit can be similar to blackberries, but the plants are smaller, or can be more bush-like, depending on the variety. Raspberries come in summer-bearing varieties, which fruit on second-year canes, or everbearing (or "fall-bearing") varieties, which produce fruit on both first- and second-year canes, allowing for multiple harvests in a season. They prefer well-drained soil, a sunny spot, and require regular pruning to maintain a healthy, productive growth habit.

Freeze-dried raspberries

Varieties

Our favorite raspberry varieties include 'Boyne' and 'Caroline' raspberries, though there are several other varieties that work for preservation purposes. It's always good to research berry varieties that will do well in your area: some are more tolerant of cold or heat than others, or they may prefer more or less humid environments.

Wild black raspberries are common here in the Midwestern United States. They're a summer-bearing variety and grow on their own. Telling the difference between wild blackberries and these black raspberries is simple. The black raspberries' leaves have white undersides, and their canes have a white film on them. Raspberries also come off hollow when picked, where blackberries keep the middle part of the berry when you pick them.

Preservation

On average, one raspberry plant can yield about 1 to 2 quarts (552 g to 1.1 kg) of berries per season, with more established plants producing even more. For a modest supply of raspberries for preserves, jams, and freezing, aim to grow ten to fifteen plants per person. Consider factors like plant variety (summer-bearing or everbearing) and growing conditions, as these can impact yield and how frequently you'll be able to harvest. We have both everbearing and summer-bearing varieties on our farm and have only ever had enough to preserve the summer-bearing varieties, which is why we recommend them for preserving purposes—though you can freeze the everbearing berries and make jams, or whatever other product, from frozen berries when you have enough. Aside from jams, jellies, and freezing, we also love to freeze-dry raspberries.

OUR FAVORITE NO-PECTIN BERRY JAM

There's nothing like fresh jam on a warm slice of toast. For this recipe, you can use raspberries, blueberries, blackberries, strawberries, huckleberries, boysenberries, dewberries, gooseberries, loganberries, or a mixture of any of these. There is a lot of sugar in this recipe, but cutting it down will result in more of a fruit syrup rather than a jam. The syrup is great over pancakes, but we're looking for more of a jam here. If you are using blackberries or raspberries (or anything with larger seeds) but don't want seeds in your jam, run them through a strainer after you cook them. If you are using strawberries, cut the tops off first. Some people prefer to core and halve them, but we don't.

INGREDIENTS

10 to 11 cups (about 3.5 pounds [1.6 kg]) fresh or frozen berries
5 cups (1 kg) sugar
1 lemon, juice and zest

COOK THE JAM

Combine ingredients in a large (10-quart [9.5 L]), heavy-bottomed pot. A wide, shallow pan works best, if available.

Heat on medium heat until the sugar dissolves, then increase the heat to medium-high. Cook to 220°F (104°C) with a candy thermometer, or use the chilled-plate method to test your jam to see if it has gelled.

The chilled plate method is a simple way to test if your jelly or jam is ready to can. Place a small plate in the freeze for 15 to 20 minutes to chill. Once you're ready to test your jelly or jam, take the plate out of the freezer and place a small spoonful on it. After 1 to 2 minutes, run your finger across the jelly on the plate. If it wrinkles or holds its shape, it is ready to can. If it is runny and comes back together in a puddle, it is not ready. The chilled plate method works by rapidly cooling the jelly so you can tell what the consistency will be like when it's cooled.

After the sugar has dissolved and the berries have softened, use a potato masher or slotted spoon to mash the berries just enough to release some of their juices.

Blackberries ready to be processed

Continue to boil the mixture, stirring constantly to prevent the jam from burning on the bottom of the pan. The berry mixture will foam up and expand, then go back down as it cooks.

NOTE: *This is where most recipes call for you to skim the foam and discard. We always skip this step, and the foam mostly goes away on its own. The jam will go from shiny and quickly bubbling to more matte in appearance and thicker, with slower bubbling—at this point, you can test for gelling by placing a spoonful of jam on a chilled plate (chill in the freezer)—after it cools on the plate a bit, run your finger across the jam: if it runs back together it isn't ready, but if the gap remains it's ready. You can also tip the plate to see if it runs.*

TO CAN THE JAM

Add hot jam to hot pint jars leaving ¼ inch (6 mm) of headspace, and water process in a water canner for 15 minutes. Remove from the canner and let rest undisturbed for 24 hours. Remove the rim and store jars for up to one year.

Note that canned strawberries are sensitive to temperature in storage. Storing in a warm place (above 80°F [27°C]) will cause the strawberries to brown—they're still safe to eat, just ugly. I've only had an issue with this when keeping them on the top shelf in our air-conditioned pantry. Strawberry pie fillings and whole canned strawberries are more susceptible than jam, but it can still happen.

↑ Calendula blooms ready for drying

← Calendula flowers on the dehydrator tray

↓ A bowl of chamomile, to be dried for tea

Flowers are a worthy addition to any food preservation garden because they attract pollinators and beneficial insects. They're also beautiful and make people happy. Everyone always talks about planting marigolds to help ward off pests, but did you know that you can also preserve their flowers?

Dried marigolds are not only beautiful, they can be used as a natural dye. To dry marigolds (any variety), simply cut them when they're half open to just recently fully opened and hang them upside-down in a bundle, away from moisture and direct sunlight, much as you would hang-dry herbs.

For flowers like chamomile, mullein, and calendula, the best way to dry the individual flowers is on a screen. We've used paper plates in a pinch, and as long as they aren't stacked and the humidity isn't too high in the room they'll dry just fine.

If you want to use your calendula for tea, it's best to separate the petals and dry them on a screen, paper plate, or in the dehydrator. The flavor of your tea will be better than if you use the entire calendula flower.

If you're growing and drying lavender, the easiest method is to dry it in a bundle. If desired, the flowers will be easier to remove after they're dry. Use a rubber band to bundle ten to twenty stems together and hang upside-down from a wall or the ceiling at ambient temperatures.

With any of these, if you use a dehydrator, dry them around 100°F (38°C) to preserve the most color/nutritional value. If you can air-dry herbs and flowers, you'll get better results, both in color and medicinal value, compared to heating them to dry.

PRESERVING FLOWERS FOR BEAUTY

Many flowers can be preserved as sustainable home, party, or wedding decor or for gifts. If you know you want to preserve flowers for this purpose, you'll have better results if you grow flowers with this in mind. Statice, strawflowers, gomphrena, celosia, and yarrow are our favorite flowers for air-drying by hanging them upside-down.

↑ Staci with a handful of flowers ready for preservation

→ A dried flower wreath, made from flowers we grew and preserved on our farm

FREEZE-DRIED FLOWERS

We've done an extensive experimentation with freeze-drying flowers. Zinnias and sunflowers are our favorite when using this method, but any flower that can be hung dry can also be freeze-dried. When freeze-drying flowers like celosia and gomphrena, you'll get a much brighter color than with air-drying and no additional steps are needed.

Soak the zinnias or sunflowers in water or harvest them just after a good rain so the petals are damp and saturated from within. After soaking, place them face-up in a pre-chilled freeze-dryer and make sure they don't touch the bottom of the shelf that's above them. Once the automated freeze-drying cycle is complete, warm the tray, then remove them, and let them sit out at room temperature and humidity for 24 hours. They won't be as brittle and can then be handled and stored without breaking them.

After one or two days, you can stack the zinnias a few layers deep. We prefer to put a piece of paper between layers of sunflowers, as their petals will be more likely to fall out. With sunflowers, the harvest stage also matters: They should be harvested when the centers are smooth and shiny, just as the petals have completely opened but before they make pollen. Smaller, pollenless varieties like the ProCut series work best.

ACHIEVING SUCCESS

We all want to succeed. And since every person defines success differently based on their experience, needs, and goals, this is admittedly a hard chapter to write. Our purpose in this closing chapter is to arm you with what we think are important tools to have in your arsenal, ideas that haven't come up in the previous chapters.

You can employ different strategies at every stage of your gardening and food preservation journey. None of them are necessarily wrong or right, and many can be combined or applied in tandem with others. This makes the process of growing and preserving your food both a science and an art.

Healthy soil is a must for a successful preservation garden.

Soil Care

Healthy soil provides your plants with the necessary nutrients, structure, and water retention for proper growth, so soil care is essential for food production. Taking care of your soil will support beneficial microorganisms that in turn help with nutrient cycling, pest control, and soil fertility, while also preventing erosion and promoting root development. Well-managed soil enhances crop yields, improves water management, and increases resilience to pests and diseases, reducing the need for harmful chemicals.

TO TILL OR NOT TO TILL, THAT IS THE QUESTION

Many gardeners grew up tilling their garden annually and using a tiller or a hoe for regular weeding. Counter to this tradition, we now know that there are many benefits to keeping soil covered, such as reducing erosion and helping the soil hold in moisture. Similarly, there are benefits to not flipping over the soil and mixing it up every year: when the soil is disturbed through tilling, it

can damage or destroy beneficial organisms like earthworms, fungi, and bacteria, which play crucial roles in nutrient cycling and soil health. This micro ecosystem in the soil performs functions such as breaking down organic matter, improving soil structure, and enhancing nutrient availability.

Though we avoid tilling whenever possible—after eight years, we've seen positive results from not tilling our space—we recognize that tilling has some benefits: controlling certain types of weeds, improving drainage in heavily compacted soils, aerating the soil and helping it warm up faster in the spring, and offering an efficient way to distribute and incorporate organic matter. If you have healthy soil biology, however, you don't need to improve drainage, aerate soil, or incorporate organic matter, because your healthy soil biology does all those things for you. Having healthy soil can even suppress certain types of weeds.

Even if tilling isn't part of your plan, it can help speed up the process of establishing your garden. There are ways to start a garden with mulch or weed fabric, but if you're like us, there will be times when you have a last-minute need for more garden space—at that point, tilling the area first can help.

↑ A good winter snow is wonderful for soil health.

→ Crimson clover is one of our favorite cover crops.

No-Till Gardening

In a no-till garden, soil amendments are added on top of the existing soil instead of mixing it in through tilling; this avoids disturbing the soil's structure. Organic materials like compost, aged manure, mulch, or cover crops can be spread over the soil surface to improve fertility, water retention, and structure. These amendments break down gradually, enriching the soil with nutrients and encouraging beneficial microorganisms. For added benefits, you can also incorporate natural minerals like lime or gypsum if you need to adjust pH or enhance your soil texture. By keeping the soil undisturbed, these amendments work over time, promoting healthier, more sustainable plant growth.

As mentioned in the sidebar in Chapter 2 (page 32), our favorite all-purpose soil amendment is rabbit manure. Top-dressing your garden with rabbit manure is a great way to boost soil fertility and promote healthy plant growth—just be sure to follow the manure safety standards we recommend on page 32. Rabbit manure is rich in nitrogen, phosphorus, and potassium, which are all essential nutrients that support strong plant development. When spread on top of the soil, it breaks down slowly, enriching the soil with organic matter, improving water retention, and enhancing microbial activity. This natural fertilizer also promotes healthier root systems and encourages lush, productive crops.

Many people ask us about using chicken manure in the garden. We have a few problems using it as fertilizer: it's a hot manure that will burn your plants if placed directly on the garden, and it should be aged or composted for at least ninety days before spreading. We've tried top-dressing with chicken house bedding (old hay or wood shavings mixed with chicken manure) in the fall. The results were that, while the grass and weeds were lush and green, our flowers took longer to bloom. This may not be bad for growing grass or green crops, but it isn't great for fruit and vegetable production. If over-applied, chicken

manure can also cause imbalances in the soil. If you want to use chicken manure, it's best to keep up with soil testing and compost the manure with other ingredients first.

If you don't have access to manure, finding a reliable source of compost is your next best option, or you can use a combination of the two. We use manure mixed with old hay (often, it's the litter from the floor of our goat and sheep barns) and leave it in place on the empty beds for months. This allows it to compost in place on the beds, which meets the required 120 days of aging before coming into contact with food plants. When we put this material combined with rabbit poop on the rows in the fall, by spring the hay and manure will be about 75 percent broken down into a beautiful growing medium. We just fell into this method, but there are hundreds of other ways to amend no-till beds—everyone has their own method they prefer to use. Ask your neighbors or local farmers for their insights if you're stuck.

Weed Control and Prevention

We touched on this topic when we covered weed fabric and weeding in chapter 3, but let's explore weed control for a preserver's garden in a little more depth. You have a number of options for dealing with weeds. We just don't enjoy hoeing and weeding every day, but we also get no pleasure from our garden when weeds are a major issue, so sometimes we have to step up and eradicate our weeds.

KNOW YOUR WEEDS

Understanding the weeds that come up regularly can help a lot with your situation. Some "weeds" are helpful, and many aren't harmful at all. By intentionally allowing some plants to grow and cover the soil—known as a "living mulch" strategy—you'll recognize the weeds that come up as part of your overall gardening plan, not as much of a problem. Living mulch can be grown as a cover crop that you terminate when it's time to plant food crops, or you can leave it to grow as a ground cover during the growing season, between crop rows or beneath plants. No plant requires space completely for itself: plants are meant to live together. Weeds only become harmful when they spread so fast they don't allow desirable plants to grow. They literally choke them out.

COVER CROPS

Cover crops can help suppress weeds, but they can also improve your soil health, prevent erosion, and attract beneficial insects. There are several factors to consider if you want to use cover crops to suppress weeds. Primary among these are the time of year when you want to plant and your specific goals for the cover crop.

Cover crops can be an effective tool for suppressing weeds in many ways. They can outcompete weeds for light, nutrients, and moisture. Crops like buckwheat and rye grow quickly and are so dense they keep weeds from germinating. Some cover crops, like certain types of radishes, can outcompete shallow rooted weeds for nutrients and moisture. We use radishes in our raised beds around plants with deeper root systems as a type of living mulch. They germinate quickly and outcompete and shade out weeds. In a few weeks, when the intended plants for that space are bigger and can hold their own, you'll have radishes to harvest and enjoy! Daikon radishes are a good radish for cover crops: they're deeply rooted and help stabilize soil, making it harder for weeds that thrive in poor, compacted soil to grow.

Once your cover crops have been terminated—that is, you've mowed, covered, or in some cases tilled them—the decomposing organic matter creates a physical barrier like mulch, feeding the soil, conserving moisture, and reducing erosion.

Whatever weeding methods you choose, know that the process will get easier over time—every weed that you pull, prevent, or smother will fail to establish itself and create seeds. This will reduce the number of weed seeds in your soil's seed bank.

What Weeds Say About Your Soil

Being able to identify weeds, rather than just blindly eradicating them, can tell you a lot about what's going on in your soil. Think of your growing area as a living ecosystem, where the plants, the soil, the rocks are all tied together with everything else. Some elements in your garden can cause harm, but sometimes the plants will give you clues that indicate the overall health of the ecosystem.

DANDELION, PLANTAIN. Often signs of compacted soil or low fertility, these plants thrive in areas where the soil is hard and has poor drainage, indicating a need for improved soil structure.

CHICKWEED. This weed prefers moist, fertile, and slightly acidic soils. Its presence might suggest that your soil is rich in organic matter but may have poor drainage or is overly compacted.

CRABGRASS. Typically growing in soils that are low in nutrients and have poor structure, crabgrass can indicate that the soil is stressed, possibly from over-tilling or poor soil fertility.

CLOVER. Often a sign of nitrogen-rich soil—clover is a legume that fixes nitrogen—this plant can indicate that your soil may have sufficient or even excess nitrogen levels.

PURSLANE. Thriving in compacted, dry, and poor soils with low fertility, the presence of purslane can suggest that your soil may need more organic matter and better aeration.

BINDWEED. This often indicates that the soil is disturbed, frequently in areas with low organic matter or nutrient imbalances. Finding bindweed may also suggest problems with soil compaction or poor drainage.

NETTLE. Preferring nutrient-rich, moist, and slightly acidic soils, abundant nettle plants may indicate that your soil has plenty of organic matter but could benefit from better drainage.

Use Those Weeds!

Sometimes the weeds that grow wild in your garden have beneficial or medicinal properties. It's not a bad plant just because it grows wild! Here are some weeds that we love.

PLANTAIN. We love plantain. Its leaves contain compounds that offer anti-inflammatory and anti-itch properties. We harvest the leaves and make them into a salve that's great on bug bites. In a pinch, you can pick one, chew it up, and put the pulp directly on a sting or bite for instant relief.

CHICKWEED. Chickweed leaves can be used to infuse oil and make a drawing salve that helps with small splinters or abscessed hairs. Very high in iron, it can be made into a tea and taken as a treatment for anemia.

NETTLE. While coming into contact with stinging nettle is no fun—its "stings" create an instant burning sensation on the skin and can cause hives—its leaves can be (carefully) harvested, dried, and made into tea. As a powerful natural antihistamine, it's a staple in our home during allergy season.

Overall, the key to using cover crops for effective weed suppression is selecting the right species, managing them properly, and incorporating them into a well-planned rotation or system that matches the local weed pressure and growing conditions.

Cover crops won't help you in ever case, depending on the type of weeds you find in your garden. Tarping may be your best bet with grasses and weeds that grow from runners, either on the surface or underground, and those that grow a new plant from every piece of weed you chop up or break when trying to remove them, such as Bermuda grass.

TARPING

Silage tarps are thick plastic sheets used by farmers to bale silage. When placed over soil, they block sunlight, blocking the germination of weed seeds and preventing the photosynthesis of existing weeds. The tarp also creates a greenhouse effect under the plastic by warming the soil, which can accelerate decomposition of organic matter and improve soil structure. Tarps can help conserve moisture, prevent erosion, and aid in soil preparation by breaking down weeds and residue.

While weed fabric is airable, allowing moisture for the ground and encouraging evaporation, tarps seal off the ground while they're down. When you remove the tarps after a few weeks or months, the area that was covered will be a blank slate you can work with as you consider other methods of weed prevention.

There are pros and cons to this method. The pros include creating a plant-free area and effectively getting rid of stubborn grasses and weeds. After tarping, applying deep mulch, cover crops, or even weed fabric will be more successful. The cons include the lack of air circulation and moisture under the tarp, which can disrupt soil microbial activity, potentially harming beneficial soil organisms like earthworms and fungi; this is especially the case if the tarp has been left for extended periods, which may be necessary with Bermuda grass.

Weed Fabric versus Tarp

Weed fabric is not the same as tarp: while both are plastic, weed fabric is woven from strips of plastic and allows water and oxygen in and out, with a weave too tight for most weeds to permeate. Weed fabric easily controls dandelions, crabgrass, clover, pigweed, wild violet, and many other weeds and grasses.

Some weeds, like Bermuda grass, creeping Charlie, quack grass, bindweed, morning glory, and nutsedge have a reputation for being difficult or downright impossible to control with weed fabric and mulching. These weeds are either rhizomatous or have deep root systems that can bypass or grow under weed fabric. Sometimes they manage to hang on and even grow through the weave of the fabric by the end of the season. Since we don't currently own silage tarps, we use weed fabric for a few months to a whole year to reclaim an area of our garden taken over by Bermuda grass.

In our experience, weed fabric can be successful even with heavy Bermuda grass, but use the fabric with intention and understand how Bermuda grows. Since it's a semitropical grass, we try to use that to our advantage over the winter months. One of the main ways we do this is by removing the weed fabric every winter: this allows the weed fabric to last longer while also exposing the Bermuda grass to the elements instead of insulating under the weed fabric. If you live in an area where Bermuda grass or other weeds don't die over the winter, this won't be a solution for you. In general, weed fabric works best on annual weeds and those that primarily spread through seeds or surface runners. For perennials that spread via deep roots or rhizomes (like Bermuda grass and quack grass), additional control methods, such as manual removal, are often required.

When using woven plastic weed fabric, it's important to remember to burn and not cut holes for your plants. We have templates for different spacings of holes for our weed fabric, and we use a propane torch to burn holes in it.

Some of our raised beds, ready for a new planting

Growing in Raised Beds or in the Ground

How you organize your garden and what you plant there will depend on your resources. Raised beds always seem like the easy way, but this isn't necessarily the case.

RAISED BEDS

Raised beds offer several benefits for gardening, making them a popular choice among gardeners. They provide improved soil drainage, which helps prevent waterlogging and root rot. They warm up faster in the spring, extending the growing season, and raised beds also allow for better soil control, as gardeners can amend the soil with high-quality compost or organic matter, ensuring optimal conditions for plant growth. Since soil has been added to them, raised beds are not generally compacted, making it easier for plant roots to penetrate and grow. They can be harder for some garden pests to get into, and raised beds can also minimize weed pressure, as they're easier to maintain and tend to keep weeds at bay. With the added benefit of less bending and kneeling, they're particularly advantageous for people with mobility issues or for those who want a more comfortable gardening experience.

While raised beds offer many advantages, they also have some drawbacks. The initial cost of materials (such as the beds themselves), soil, and compost can be high, making it a more expensive option when starting up compared to traditional in-ground gardening. Raised beds also require more frequent watering, as the soil tends to dry out faster than in-ground beds. Over time, the soil in raised beds may need to be replenished with compost or organic matter, as it can settle or become depleted of nutrients. In our garden, we add back 25 to 50 percent of the soil or amendments to our raised beds every year just to keep them going.

IN-GROUND GARDENING

This method offers several benefits, including lower initial costs, since there's no need for building materials or special soil amendments. It allows for larger planting areas, providing more space for root growth, and can be less labor intensive than building and maintaining raised beds. Additionally, the soil often retains moisture better, especially with added mulch, reducing the need for frequent watering. In-ground gardening also allows for more natural soil structure and can support deeper root systems.

In-ground gardening has its own disadvantages to consider. The soil in your area may be compacted, poorly drained, or lacking in nutrients, requiring more effort to improve its quality. Weeds can be more difficult to control, and pests or diseases may be harder to manage. Using the no-till methods discussed earlier in this chapter can help you to build up and plant in poor soil conditions if you're committed to keeping costs and watering needs down.

Lack of funds is a motivating factor for many in-ground gardens. We always gardened in raised beds when we lived in the city and had a tiny garden. When we moved to our farm and wanted to expand our garden, we needed to learn to grow plants directly in the ground. In our case, we were extremely lucky: we found a homestead that was over 140 years old with a mature, historical garden. This meant that someone else had cleared the rocks and amended the soil for many years. The challenge was to fight back the last few decades of weeds as we got started. We've since established no-till, in-ground beds in other parts of our farm. In our experience, even year-one plants thrive in our no-till beds, but after three or four years these beds have the most beautiful soil.

We do use some raised beds in our garden too. We try to leverage the positive aspects where they help us: peppers grow better in raised beds in our garden, for example; while our in-ground soil can get soggy in the spring, the faster-draining soil in our raised beds helps the pepper plants to thrive. Our younger children (aged ten and under) each have their own raised bed for their own gardening experiments. While this could be done in-ground, it's easier for learning minds to visualize the borders of the raised beds when planning and growing their own garden. It's fun and fulfilling to watch them plan their garden and take it all the way through to harvest.

Organizing Your Preservation Garden

A new garden requires planning to ensure optimal growth and ease of maintenance. Here's a task checklist for setting up a garden from scratch:

- Start by assessing your garden site.
- Consider factors like sunlight, soil quality, and drainage.
- Choose a layout that maximizes sunlight exposure, with taller plants or structures placed to the north and shorter plants to the south (in the Northern Hemisphere).
- Create plant groupings based on their water, light, and soil needs.
- Plan for efficient irrigation, pathways for easy access, and ample space between plants for airflow and growth.

Remember that your garden is a living thing, and most of the plants you put there (except some berry plants and trees) are probably annuals. That means you can decide to move things around and shift plans with each new planting season. Set aside time for an annual or quarterly planning session to evaluate how things are going and make any necessary adjustments for the next period. Keep a journal of gardening thoughts and ideas—even take notes on your phone so you can access them easily.

SEED STARTING VERSUS PLANT STARTS

Should you start your own seeds or purchase plant starts? That depends a lot on your experience, how much time and money you have to invest in your garden, and what local resources are available.

It can be hard to justify the cost of high-quality plant starts when you're growing a large garden. You can get around this by buying plant starts

A healthy start in our greenhouse

from a local farmer or produce auctions; we've found plant starts in the spring at the same auctions where we buy produce we can't grow ourselves. Many small farms and market gardeners who sell produce also grow extra plants to sell in the spring. Purchasing plant starts from proven growers like this helps you and the growers: you know that you're getting the same varieties that they're growing for high production, the plants you buy will be healthy and locally grown, and you'll be supporting a local farm. If this is your first attempt or you don't have a great setup for starting seeds indoors, try buying plant starts—just don't buy them from the big-box stores.

When you buy plants or seeds for your garden, you don't have to treat it like an all-or-nothing commitment. Before we built our greenhouses and started growing most of our plants from seed, we didn't have room to start plants in our small, crowded home, so we bought plants that required a lot of time indoors before being planted out: peppers, tomatoes, and onions. We still purchase our onion starts, because we don't want to have plants growing in December when we could buy them and otherwise wait until February to get started.

Many gardeners direct-seed squash, cucumbers, peas, and lettuce—produce that we like to start in our greenhouse—but plants like this only need to be started a couple weeks before or can be seeded directly. This method has many pros and cons. The benefits of direct-seeding include only touching the baby plant or seed once (which means less work) and establishing a stronger root system with no risk of transplant shock. Cons include more vulnerability to pest pressure and a shorter growing season. When we put a squash seed into a mound of dirt, it seems like every squirrel in the area thinks we're putting out treats for them! Other methods like low tunnels can be employed to help warm the soil early and allow for earlier, direct sowing along with some protection from early pest damage.

↑ Baby pumpkin plants in our greenhouse

↓ Staci in front of her baby plant starts

GREENHOUSE, HIGH TUNNELS, AND STARTING PLANTS INDOORS

For a small-scale gardener, starting plants indoors with grow lights is often more manageable than in a greenhouse. You may dream of a greenhouse or high tunnel to start your plants in, but there's a lot more to building and maintaining these structures than you might think.

Before deciding on a greenhouse or a high tunnel, it is important to understand the difference between the two. Essentially, they are (or can be) the same thing, with the high-level difference being that a greenhouse is a more permanent, rigid structure with climate control features such as heaters and fans, and high tunnels are typically considered to be less permanent and reliant only on the environment for heating and cooling.

For one thing, your climate will have a bearing on how helpful a greenhouse or high tunnel can be. While high tunnels (also known as hoop houses) offer protection from the elements for growing plants, they're typically unheated, and greenhouses are more likely to have heating systems. High tunnels and unheated greenhouses receive the sun's heat during the day, but by morning the temperatures inside typically drop to the same as the outdoor temperature. Heated greenhouses, however, offer year-round climate control.

Size matters too: the smaller the structure, the faster its temperature will drop at night. A large high tunnel with plants in the ground will maintain a higher overnight temperature than a small unheated greenhouse, but there's no guarantee that the inside temperature will stay above freezing. It's also important to remember that every layer of plastic on greenhouses and high tunnels buys you a little more heat, typically about 5°F (–15°C). We put low tunnels (a mini version of a high tunnel) inside our greenhouses because they create smaller spaces that are easier and cheaper to heat, which in turn gives us more temperature control on cold nights. Tomatoes and peppers need temperatures over 50°F (10°C) at night, so a March start inside a greenhouse in Missouri requires added heat and two layers of plastic, in addition to a heat source to maintain this temperature. Starting seeds of those same crops in an unheated high tunnel in March would not work in our climate.

When we put up our first greenhouse, we only expected to grow plants for our family. We wound up with more plants than we had expected, which we sold as a way to cover the cost of maintaining the greenhouse and buying more supplies.

A lot of effort goes into growing plants in a greenhouse: daily monitoring of temperatures, humidity, and soil moisture; turning fans on and off; and opening and closing vents and windows. There are ways to automate these checks and adjustments (another added cost), but when the seedlings start coming on our farm, we can't leave the property for more than an hour or two: the sun might go behind a cloud, or the temperature inside the greenhouse might get hotter than we want. We choose to control the interior temperature manually during the day, but we use heaters set on a thermostat for nighttime regulation. This is the most efficient way to keep overnight temperatures stable. We also have different zones and different greenhouses based on the plants that need to be kept at different temperatures. While tomatoes and peppers need to stay above 50°F (10°C), many other crops can tolerate temperatures down near freezing.

Before going to the trouble of building and heating a greenhouse, consider starting your plants indoors. You can easily grow fifty or one hundred tomato plants in a relatively small space inside your house with grow lights and shelves.

In summary, if you're considering a greenhouse or high tunnel, make sure to do more research than we did before you start! Your goals, climate conditions, and scale will be factors to consider.

← Trays of mixed spring vegetable starts in the greenhouse

BENEFICIAL INSECTS

Common garden (orb) spider

Baby praying mantis

Earthworms in our no-till soil

Black swallowtail caterpillars

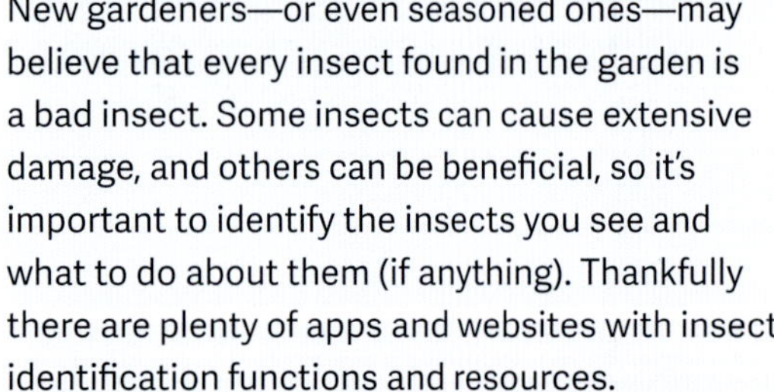

New gardeners—or even seasoned ones—may believe that every insect found in the garden is a bad insect. Some insects can cause extensive damage, and others can be beneficial, so it's important to identify the insects you see and what to do about them (if anything). Thankfully there are plenty of apps and websites with insect identification functions and resources.

The first rule is to be observant, then to do your research and be sure of what you've seen before trying to remove an insect in your garden. You might find black swallowtail caterpillars munching on your dill (see page 116)—they're a beneficial insect, but maybe not the best if you want to preserve your dill plants, so relocate them to a different part of your garden. Ladybugs (and their larvae), praying mantis, green lacewings, and parasitic wasps are examples of beneficial insects that hunt potentially harmful pests and keep them in check. Learn about the insects in your garden and learn about which ones you can actually *introduce* to improve your situation. We've purchased eggs and larvae for ladybugs and praying mantis, which has had wonderful results for our plants: both insects thrive on aphids and many other nasty bugs.

Team Gardening

There are a number of ways you work with other people to share in gardening tasks. Team gardening can mean sharing a space, sharing responsibilities, or taking turns checking each other's garden. Some plants don't grow well at our farm, but we have friends nearby who have greater success. We work out a deal to swap produce with our friends, supply them with items from our farm in exchange for what they can give us, making for a win-win arrangement.

Your neighbors are a great source of support: you can offer to work in their garden (or loan out your kids to help), or you can share your experience and insights about growing specific plants. Help an elderly neighbor or friend with their garden in exchange for their knowledge. Maybe they can decide to grow pumpkins and you'll grow tomatoes, then you can swap the produce when it's ready. The sky's the limit on what you can accomplish when you team up with other farmers and gardeners.

Community Gardens

A community garden will be somewhere away from your own growing space, possibly miles away, which may not give you enough time for daily walkthroughs. We participated in a community garden for several years before investing in garden beds at our house in town. While it was inconvenient, it gave us a space to learn, working with compost and soil in a raised bed that was already set up for us. Though we lost some produce to the local wildlife, it was ultimately a positive experience, giving us an opportunity to learn from other gardeners with neighboring plots. Community gardens are often a great way to meet that gardening friends or mentors.

Companion Planting

As we mentioned in chapter 3, proper companion planning can have a positive effect on the amount you produce and the quality of your harvests. You'll be using your space more efficiently and see increased yields thanks to synergistic plant relationships.

While nice, neat garden rows and beds appeal to us as humans, mixing things up can be more beneficial. Companion planting helps deter pests, improve growth, and reduce the need for chemical pesticides. You can also seriously increase your garden size.

Shade and Shelter

Shade and shelter are essential in the summer to protect your garden from heat and prevent plants from wilting or suffering sunburn. Your climate will dictate how you should approach this: if you live somewhere with hot summers or windy springs, you may need to take action to protect your plants. This can be something as simple as placing your garden in a location where it gets eight hours of sun with shade from a building or trees, instead of full sun from sunrise to sunset every day in the middle of summer. Intense sun can cause soil to dry out quickly, stressing plants and stunting their growth. Providing shade through trees, trellises, or shade cloth helps maintain cooler soil temperatures, conserving moisture and reducing water stress. Shelter from winds or intense sun allows plants to focus their energy on growing rather than struggling to survive, and this can lead to healthier, more productive crops. It's a simple way to ensure that your garden thrives even in the hottest months.

Providing shade and shelter in your garden doesn't have to involve buying expensive materials. You can easily use items you already have lying around. Here are a few DIY methods.

- Old bed sheets or fabric: Stretch an old sheet, tarp, or lightweight fabric across stakes or a DIY frame to create a simple shade cloth. You can also use an old shower curtain or tablecloth if it's light enough to allow some sun to filter through.
- Recycled pallets: If you have wooden pallets, stack them vertically or lean them against a wall to create a makeshift trellis or shade structure. Add a tarp or fabric to the top for more coverage.
- Tree branches or shrubs: If you have overgrown shrubs, vines, or tree branches, let them grow to create natural shade. Fast-growing, vine-plants like beans or cucumbers on a trellis will also work to provide shade as they grow.
- Garden umbrella or old patio furniture: If you have an unused patio umbrella or outdoor furniture with a large canopy, repurpose it in your garden for shade. Just move it where you need protection from the sun.
- Upcycled window screens: Old window screens can be mounted on stakes to act as a windbreak or partial shade. They allow light through but can also block strong winds and intense sun.
- Reclaimed wood or bamboo poles: Use leftover wood, bamboo poles, or even sturdy branches to create a frame, then drape a piece of fabric, burlap, or an old shower curtain over the construction for shade.
- Recycled plastic bottles or jugs: Cut the bottoms off large plastic bottles and bury them halfway in the ground to create little shaded areas or mini greenhouses for small plants.

Be Thoughtful

Maybe you want to combine weed fabric with companion planting and cover crops. We have a couple options in our garden. Weed fabric goes in the aisles of our tomato rows, with a 4-inch (10 cm) gap between the fabric under our trellis. In this gap we plant our tomatoes along with basil, onions, garlic, dill, and occasionally peas and beans (not all of these plants play well together, but in our experience they help our tomatoes). Our garden still looks neat and tidy with these rows of various plants living together.

In our flower field, where our rows are all 4 feet (1.2 m) wide, we add various lengths of fabric with pre-burned holes spaced apart 6, 9, or 12 inches (15, 23, or 30 cm). We interplant things that can benefit each other and have similar growth habits and water needs. This helps give the look of an organized garden with the varied, pest-deterrent ecosystem benefits that come with not planting the same flowers over a large area.

We also use containers to add variety with companion plants in our in-ground vegetable garden. Herbs that deter pests and attract beneficial insects like basil, oregano, dill, mint, cilantro, chamomile, and many others do very well in ten-gallon (38 L) containers in the garden.

Keep Realistic Expectations

Whether you're new to gardening or have been doing it for years, keeping your expectations realistic is important. Remember:

- You won't have a good year every year.
- You won't grow everything you need every year.
- You can't control everything.
- Sometimes crops will fail or underproduce.

Success isn't always guaranteed! If this were easy, everyone would do it. Know that, while your results will improve as you garden year over year, any setbacks you experience will be new learning opportunities.

YIN AND YANG

In the garden, every action has a reaction, and every positive has a negative.

→ Hail damage to leafy plants can be stunting, if not fatal, to the plant.

- Mild winters mean more bugs next year.
- Lots of rain can mean mildew and root rot.
- An amazing yield may mean you need to replenish your soil more than usual next season.

As with so much in life, these outcomes aren't necessarily bad—they're reality. Understanding this can be the difference between those who succeed and those who fail.

Weather Preparedness

What happens if your garden is destroyed by hail, a windstorm, or a late frost?

HAIL

Every climate is different, and your potential for getting hail is different than mine. You have to decide if the risk is worth it. One quick storm of

Hail: every gardener's nightmare

pea-sized hail can decimate your garden, so the threat is real. Consider hail netting if you live somewhere where hail is typical, or you may lose your garden.

WIND

Good trellising is key to keeping your plants upright in a strong wind. It's hard to comprehend the force of wind on vining plants: Each leaf acts as a sail, and the force can be amazingly strong. For our tomatoes, for example, we use heavy-gauge cattle panels connected to 8-foot (2.4 m) T-posts held on by metal hose clamps. In the spring, this looks like overkill, but if you lose your entire crop to a freak windstorm, this setup will make perfect sense.

FLOODING

Don't plant your garden in an area that floods. If you must plant in a low spot, raised beds could help it drain faster. Knowing your property and how it responds to heavy rains before you choose your garden's location can help. When you choose an area for your garden, keep in mind that it may not flood in its current state, but after you move dirt and make rows flooding may be more likely. Proper drainage is key.

LATE FROST

Know your microclimate. Use remote thermometers to monitor the garden temperature to be aware of changes, such as your garden's air becoming colder than the forecast low in your area. There are inexpensive Bluetooth and Wi-Fi thermometers that can keep records for you and show you trends. We can look at forecast temperatures on the local news and guess with pretty good certainty that a low on a given night will be *X* degrees lower than what was predicted.

Always Have a Backup Plan

When we first plant out our tomato starts, we always keep a few back in the greenhouse in case something happens to the first planting. One year we had a hailstorm a day or two after we'd planted our first ninety tomato plants. We were lucky—the hail was only the size of quarters, which was large enough to knock down two of my new tomato starts—but a smaller hail would have shredded them. We were able to root the broken plants and replant them later, but we also had extras left in the greenhouse to replace them. This is partly because we were growing a lot of plants for an on-farm plant sale we run every year. But even before we were selling thousands of plants every year, we always grew a few extras. If we didn't need them, we could always give them away or find a spot for them.

Once all my tomato plants are in the ground, we prune them once a week (as covered in the tomato produce profile in chapter 2). When pruning suckers off the tomatoes, we keep a few of the sturdiest, largest suckers (branches) and root them in 1 cup (250 ml) of water. Once rooted, they go into small pots. This can either be your next succession of tomato plants, or they can be your disaster plan in case your garden sustains damage in the first month and you lose plants.

With other crops, like beans, corn, lettuce, and so on, succession planting can give your plants the best chance of survival in unexpected weather.

Gardening puts you at risk for many challenges that are out of your control, from weather to fire to damaging wildlife. Above all, grow more than you need season to season if you can. We always try to grow a bit of extra food for long-term storage to avoid running out of basics like tomato sauce. Refer to chapter 2 for planning your food storage needs, and keep any potential calamities in mind when you decide how much food to keep on hand.

Final Tips for Success

Be present in your garden every day. Daily walkthroughs are a must. If you're a seasoned gardener, you'll know your soil, know what you're planting, and know when it will be ready to harvest. Your walkthroughs will take less time as you build your awareness and expertise. When the harvest is slowing down and we're on the other side of peak gardening season, we'll do a walkthrough so quickly it can hardly be considered a check; that's because we know our soil, weather, and plants well enough to evaluate the situation quickly and then spend our time focusing on other tasks.

Pay attention to the weather: This is important when planting, but it also holds for your daily tasks. If a storm is coming, you don't need to water, but you do need to make sure everything is properly trellised and that your tomatoes are tied up, or they may not make it through the storm. If there's a stretch of miserable weather coming, but three days later it's forecast to be clear and beautiful, plan to spend extra time the day before the weather turns nasty: this will save some of your work the day after the storm passes. This is a more efficient approach, and it will help you look forward to something that you may have otherwise quietly dreaded.

Know yourself. Find ways to motivate yourself and stay on track. Create a schedule or routine, find a garden buddy to share your successes and failures with and to challenge you. Weigh your produce and try to beat your own records if that motivates you. Figure out what motivates you and play to your strengths.

About the Authors

STACI AND JEREMY HILL are the owners of Gooseberry Bridge Farm (@gooseberrybridgefarm), located in the Ozark Mountains of southwestern Missouri. They moved from the typical "house at the end of a cul-de-sac in a subdivision" to a 11.6-acre (4.7-ha) farm almost ten years ago—and they haven't looked back! In addition to producing and preserving as much of their own foods as possible by canning, freezing, dehydrating, and freeze-drying their garden harvests, they also operate a you-pick flower farm with different varieties of flowers throughout the year. Their goals are to share their farm with the community and to be as self-sufficient as possible within the boundaries of what is realistic in today's world.

Acknowledgments

A project like writing a book is a bit like planting a single squash vine and thinking it'll stay in its lane—it quickly takes over everything, demands your full attention, and somehow ends up climbing the fence. But with enough support, it produces something you're actually proud of.

Writing a book about gardening and food preservation seemed like a great idea—until we tried doing it during actual gardening and preserving season. Still, between the chaos, the canning, and the compost, something took shape. And to our surprise, it wasn't a disaster. Of course, it wasn't just us. We had a lot of help and couldn't have done this without a lot of amazing people.

To our six amazing kids: Thank you for being part of this every step of the way. Mollie, you've become a food preservation wizard, picking up the jar-lifters and taking over the kitchen when we're buried in the harvest. Also, thanks for being a semi-willing model for book photos. Jamie, thank you for tackling the dishes and the freeze-dryer trays without (much) complaint—we see you, and we appreciate you. Annie, thank you for being a steady hand in the garden, even when you'd really rather be crocheting. Your hard work has made a big impact, especially for someone who doesn't like veggies. And to Bently, Robin, and Teddy—our enthusiastic rabbit wranglers and garden buddies—you are our right hands out there, turning chores into something (almost) fun. The garden is greener because of you.

To Alex: Thank you for the heavy lifting—literally and figuratively. Whether it's hauling feed in the barn or fixing what no one else wants to touch, you keep everything standing—plants, fences, and sometimes people.

Kelly, thank you for all of your support and for getting your hands dirty potting up tomato and pepper seedlings—and so much more. We couldn't have made it through the last few seasons without you.

To our parents: Thank you for your constant support, your encouragement, and your help with the kids. We are amazingly lucky to have the support structure that we have in you.

Thank you to Grandpa Steve for being our resident carpenter, building our greenhouses with the kind of precision and patience we can only aspire to.

To Grandpa James: Thank you for sharing your gardening wisdom over the years—the cattle panel tomato trellising and other tips have made all the difference.

To Grandma Barb: Thank you for always being there, and for making sure we got our freeze dryer. We wouldn't have made the leap without you and it has changed everything.

To Grandma Lynda: Thank you for always greeting our farm customers with a smile, and helping wrangle the boys.

To our friend Rick: Thank you for always being there for questions and legal advice. We're still figuring out how to repay you in pickles.

To our editors and publishing team: Thank you for believing we could actually do this, and for patiently answering every one of our newbie author questions along the way. Turns out, we weren't as bad at this as we thought—and that's largely thanks to you.

And to our loyal social media followers: Thank you for cheering us on, asking smart questions, sharing your garden wins and canning mishaps, and for reminding us (repeatedly) that one good earthquake could turn our entire pantry into a pile of broken glass. The shelves are solid ... but they have no lip, no rope, and no backup plan. It's a risk we're willing to take.

To every backyard gardener, canning convert, and person staring down a bushel of produce with wide eyes and sticky hands: This book is for you. May your seeds sprout, your jars seal, and your neighbors always say yes to "just a few extra zucchini."

Index